The Art and Skill

of Talking
With People

The Art and Skill

A NEW GUIDE
TO PERSONAL AND BUSINESS
SUCCESS

Englewood Cliffs, N.J.

# of Talking
With People

by Hugh P. Fellows, Ph.D.

Illustrations by Charles Miller

Prentice-Hall, Inc.

PRINTED IN THE UNITED STATES OF AMERICA

04686—B&P

What This Book Can Do for You

THE *Art and Skill of Talking With People* can help you to improve your skill in talking with others and, consequently, your human relations, in a business or social conversation, in a conference, on the telephone and in making a public speech. Primarily, it is a practical guide for the young business executive, or aspiring executive. The more mature business or professional man or woman will also find the book useful in learning to meet speech situations with ease.

Why do you, a progressing business man, need a book of this nature? Because your ability to speak well is *your most important single asset* in business and society. You spend about three-fourths of your waking hours in some form of communication. In school you have taken courses in writing, and perhaps a course or two in reading; yet you may have gone through college or even graduate school without a single course in listening and speaking—the activities which consume most of your time! This book can make you a more skilful listener and speaker.

The techniques suggested by this book are definite. They have been tested and found effective over a period of more than twenty years by executives and supervisors in large business corporations, professional men and women, legislators, officers in the armed forces, safety engineers, teachers and college students. Because I realize that I am writing for busy people who are often tired when they find time to read, I have tried to write with brevity and breeziness. However, this is not a book about chit-chat over pre-luncheon martinis or in the country club locker room.

Three Steps to Your Goal

Cicero, the Roman statesman and orator, said that diligence is only a single virtue, but one in which all other virtues are comprehended. So, be diligent. To accomplish any degree of self improvement, you must go through three stages:

Realization of your need

Admittedly, there are many people who loaf on their jobs and who don't care whether or not they do a good job so long as they get paid, but there are *hundreds of thousands* of people who function poorly because they are *not aware* of their incompetence. They don't really *desire* to do a job poorly (as many supervisors suspect!); they simply do not *know* that they *are* doing poorly. A high school junior was sent to me by his parents for help with his enunciation. "He slurs all his words so dreadfully that we can hardly understand him," the parents complained. The boy was dutiful and polite, but obviously uninterested in improving his diction. After I had established some *rapport* with him, he confided (I won't attempt to spell the way he sounded!), "I don't see why Mom and Dad want to send me here. I talk like all the other kids at school. *They* don't have any trouble understanding me. Most of my teachers don't complain about the way I talk, 'cause I talk like everybody else. What's all the fuss about?"

He had a point; he didn't want to be different from his peers, and I could understand that.

"If you could be sure that you would remain sixteen years old all your life, and that you would always associate only with the kids at school, there'd be no need for improving your speech. However, if you will listen to the way people speak on radio and television—men who have accomplished something—and compare it with the way the kids speak, I think you'll hear a difference. Remember that you will have to be dealing with such people some day, and I believe that you'll understand why your parents want you to improve your speech."

He responded, worked diligently, and improved his diction to a point where he and his parents were delighted.

If you have chosen this book, the odds are that you have realized a lack in your ability to talk well with others, so you are already at this stage. Now let us contemplate what is ahead.

Trials without fear

After you have learned what to do and how to do it, you may try it and fail. Don't be discouraged. Even after you have learned a skill, there will be times when you lapse into old habits. This is the uncomfortable stage when you have to *think* before applying a skill that has been acquired recently. First, you think *after* you have spoken ("I wish I hadn't said it that way!"), and then you think *before* you speak ("Now, I must be careful!"); in either instance, it's an awkward situation. This is the stage when practice becomes important to *set* a pattern and form a habit of doing something as it should be done.

Unconscious skill

Having learned how to speak well, and having practiced enough to form a habit of it, you now reach the blissful stage when you *know* you are going to speak competently on any occasion. Oh, sometimes you may lapse into old habits, but these lapses are likely to occur only when you're excessively tired, excited or intoxicated. I hope that relapses from these causes will be few! If speaking well is a "consummation devoutly to be wished" for you, you can do more than merely wish for it, if you use this book properly.

How to Use This Book

The Art and Skill of Talking With People is divided into three parts. Part One has been written to give you an understanding of the nature of oral communication. I have described some of the ways misunderstandings arise when we talk with others, and how to avoid such misunderstandings. All of the chapters in Part One are concerned with your speech personality as it exhibits itself when you speak. One chapter contains practical suggestions for helping you overcome self-consciousness and stage fright, and for utilizing nervous energy to your advantage.

Part Two is devoted to two speech activities in which we all engage daily—conversation and telephone conversation. These two chapters contain material based on practical research over many years, and tested in workshops with business and professional men and women. It is an unorthodox approach to these subjects, and I believe that you will find answers to questions which no other book has attempted to answer.

Part Three is a practical book of information on mastering group speech situations: How to participate in a public discussion or problem-solving conference, how to hold a meeting, how to organize a symposium and how to put into practice parliamentary procedure. Some pages are "stodgy" because of the nature of the material, but I have tried to "perk up" the information wherever possible. Anyway, give it a try!

My first suggestion for using this book is that you read it leisurely. Read a chapter from Part One and allow a couple of days to go by before reading the next chapter. Give yourself time to *observe* and *think about* how the principles set forth in that chapter operate in daily life. If you do this, your social and business worlds become your classrooms. This book is closely related to the world and the people around you; if you observe its principles in action, they will leave an indelible impression on your mind.

If you have a special problem, turn to the chapter dealing with that problem; you will find that each chapter is complete within itself. If your problem is stage fright, read the chapter on "Self-Confidence," and let the suggestions in it start working for you right away. If you are about to participate in your first problem-solving conference, a few minutes' study of Chapter Ten will outline procedure and give you the assurance that you will be using a method that has been tested successfully in literally hundreds of conferences.

This book has been prepared to be *useful*. Use it!

Contents

Part One

Your Personal Equipment

Part Two

Person to Person

The Art
and Skill

of Talking
With People

P_{art} O_{ne}

Your Personal Equipment

Chapter One

Understanding
One Another

AS long as men have business and desires, misunderstandings are sure to arise. However, we can strive to lessen those misunderstandings in both business and social life; that is what this book will try to do. There are four major barriers to successful communication among people: (a) semantic difficulties, (b) psychological differences, (c) poor listening and (d) unskilled organization. These barriers overlap frequently; many times it is not possible to talk about one without taking others into consideration. However, let us try to isolate the first two and examine them in this chapter.

Semantic Difficulties

General semantics may be described as a study of how to deliver an adequate representation of facts and events, how to evaluate properly those facts and events, and how to understand others' evaluation of events, happenings and objects. Whew! That's a pretty big order, isn't it? It takes in more than the scope of this entire book. S. I. Hayakawa, of the University of San Francisco, defines general semantics as "the study of how not to be a damn fool!" [1] That, too, takes in more than the scope of this book. However, let us be ambitious enough to say that this chapter will offer some suggestions for not being a damn fool in at least a few ways. First, let's try not to be damned fools about words themselves.

Multiple meanings

When someone tells you that he spoke in "plain, simple English," he may be grossly misrepresenting the fact. English is rarely simple or plain, as you can demonstrate for yourself.

Say aloud the word "see" to a friend (don't spell it), and ask him to guess what you mean by it. He has many choices; here are just a few:

1. A body of water (sea).
2. A letter in the alphabet (C).
3. A musical note (e.g., C-sharp).
4. To understand something ("Do you see?").
5. The affirmative in Spanish ("Sí"—but it can also mean "if" in Spanish!).
6. A bishop's seat of power (The Holy See).
7. To investigate something ("Run and see what he's doing").
8. A proper name (Seay).
9. To use one's eyes (Isn't that what everyone does?).

All nine of the above words, while spelled differently in some cases, are pronounced alike and take on different meanings in different contexts.

---

[1] *Life,* October 19, 1962, p. 102.

Take another example. I think you'll agree that, to most people, the word "up" indicates the direction towards the sky, and that "down" indicates the direction towards the earth. Now, read the following quotations and answer the question following each:

1. "Dan came *down* with a cold and has been laid *up* for a week." Is Dan down or up?

2. "If they shut *down* this school, will they keep it closed *up?*"

"Aw, pipe *down!* I mean, shut *up!*"

"But, if they've closed *down* the school and intend to keep it shut *up*, will the pupils come *down* to find that none of the teachers has shown *up?*"

Just where *will* the pupils go—up or down?

3. "Arthur, you're driving too fast; slow *up*," cautioned his wife. "Yes, Daddy, please slow *down!*" rejoined his daughter. Will Arthur lose control of his automobile?

If I tell you that I'm going to "take some soda," it might mean that I'm going to drink a refreshing drink, flavored with strawberry or some other syrup; or, it might mean that I have indigestion and am going to take a teaspoonful of bicarbonate of soda mixed with a little water. However, if I tell you that I'm going to take a dose of $NaHCO_3$, you can be sure that I mean bicarbonate of soda. $NaHCO_3$ is a technical word, and technical words attempt to be precise (even *they* are not sacred cows when it comes to having more than one meaning). However, out of the 750,000 words that comprise the English language, only about 150,000 are technical words; that leaves us about 600,000 words which may have more than one meaning. See how many meanings you can find for the following: *stand, strike, salt, back, table, plug* and *go*. A check through the *Oxford English Dictionary* for the different senses in which they may be used will reveal that more than *thirty* different meanings may be found for each of these common prepositions: *with, at, to, by, for, on, of, from* and *in!*

When using words to communicate meaning, be sure that you and your listener have the same *meaning* in mind.

Regional differences

Consider the following conversation:

SOUTHERNER: Just before writing this chapter, I took a dope.

SOCIAL WORKER: He means that he gave shelter to some poor person who is not mentally alert.

STUDENT: He does not. He means that he's full of knowledge on the subject. All right, doc; what's the dope?

SOUTHERNER: Perhaps the word "took" is misleading; I should have said, "I *had* a dope before writing this."

LIMEY: Aaow, guv'nor! D'ye always have to seduce some poor girl wot's not got all 'er wits about 'er, before you writes?

SOUTHERNER: No, no! I mean that I *drank* a dope.

SOCIAL WORKER: Narcotics? Poor man!

NEW YORKER: Aw, cut it out! All he means is that he drank Coke before writing.

COAL MINER: Anybody knows you can't *drink* coke! What kind of talk is that?

BRITISHER: I say, you *are* dense, aren't you? After all, the man merely said he drank a squash.

GARDENER: *Drank* a squash! How could he?

NEW ENGLANDER: Is there anything wrong with his having a bottle of pop?

BRITISHER: Oh! So your father's passing out bottles now?

And all the time, the southerner was talking about Coca-Cola! All the time, also, English was being spoken, but it meant something different to people from different localities. When a young lady in England tells you that she is "knocked up," it does not necessarily mean that she is pregnant—not even slightly—but that she is fatigued. And if an Australian girl refuses a date with you on a Friday afternoon because that's the afternoon she "must get screwed," she is not being lewd; she is merely going to collect

her week's salary. Several years ago, there was a Broadway play entitled *Papa Is All*; it did not mean that Papa was everything; it meant, instead, that Papa was finished and done with. The play was about the Pennsylvania Dutch, to whom the word "all" means finished. And, of course, I don't need to remind you that while the adjective "bloody" is not offensive to an American, it still is not used in polite society in England.

So, another difficulty in communicating with words—at least with English words—is that they are apt to mean different things in different places where English is spoken.

Words are also apt to take on different meanings for different people according to the manner in which they are exposed to them. Consider this example:

Just after one of the teen-age gang wars in New York City, the driver of the taxicab in which I was riding started a discussion of young people of today. Our conversation took the usual pessimistic view which most older people adopt when discussing a younger generation. The driver remarked, "I tell ya one t'ing: I gotta kid he's ten years old. If 'e grows up to be a yewt, I'm gonna cut 'is t'roat!"

I was puzzled. I understood his threat of cutting the boy's throat, but the only "yewt" I could think of was a Ute Indian. Perhaps he meant a yewt—a salamander—but it still didn't make sense. I asked him to repeat what he had said, and he obliged, but I remained baffled. Finally, I asked outright,

"Excuse me, but what is a 'yewt'?"

"Aah, *you* know! Ya read it in da papers alla time: 'Yewt kills goil,' 'Yewt robs candy store,' 'Yewt steals car.' I'm tellin ya, if my kid grows up to be one o' dem yewts, I'm gonna kill 'im."

Then I understood: a "yewt" was a "youth"! The startling thing to me was that, because of headlines in the tabloid newspapers, the only thing that the word "youth" represented to that taxicab driver was a criminal!

In using words—and in listening to them—try to find out if they mean the same thing to you as to someone in a different locality.

Time changes

When I was a teen-ager, a vivacious, attractive, well-dressed girl was called "hot stuff!" Today, that same young creature might be referred to as a "cool cat"! Also, while I was growing up, the expression "Give her the gun!" could only mean delivering a firearm to a female; today it means accelerating the throttle on an automobile or airplane. To give you an idea of how completely some words have changed in meaning over the years, let's introduce a twentieth-century student of communications to a medieval king.

MR. I.Q.: Your majesty, I have a complaint to make against Lawrence Longhair; he was very rude to me.

KING: What! Where did he hurt you?

I.Q.: Oh, he didn't touch me. In my century to be rude is to be impolite.

KING: I see. Well, I'm surprised. Lawrence Longhair is a most worthy and gentle villain.

I.Q.: Worthy and gentle villain? How can your majesty contradict your majesty?

KING: Contradict? *Je ne sais pas!* [2]

I.Q.: A villain is a scoundrel, a blackguard, a gangster. You know, like Public Enemy Number One.

KING: My dear boy, a villain is someone who lives in a villa.

I.Q.: Yeah, that's what I mean. He probably stole it!

KING: How now, gossip. Would you like to live in a villa?

I.Q.: You mean sixteen baths and fourteen rooms? Sure I would! But what's this "gossip" stuff? I'm not gossiping; I know when somebody's been rude to me.

KING: Gossip? Why, that simply means a kinsman, one "related in God." But Lawrence Longhair is not a scoundrel, simply because he is a villain; why, the poor man works so hard that he is obese.

I.Q.: Obese? Why, he's as skinny as a rail.

KING: That's what I mean—wasted, eaten away. Isn't that what obese means in your century?

I.Q.: Of course not; now you're just being silly.

KING: I pray earnestly that I may be.

I.Q. (*unbelievingly*): Wh-a-a-t?

KING: Why, yes; silly comes from the word *selig*, which means blessed, or happy. But I would be gorgeous [3] if I claimed to be that.

I.Q.: Gorgeous? You're as homely as a mud fence! But what's all this got to do with Lawrence Longhair and his villainy?

KING: Lawrence is a villain because he lives in a villa, which is only a poor farm hut in my century.

---

[2] Well, they may as well have spoken French so far as communication was concerned.

[3] Originally meant "proud."

I.Q.: Well, I don't like the way he talks. He just told me to bring my Yankee sweetheart to him and he'd give her some fool. Now, everybody knows my sweetheart is a Scotswoman, not a Yankee, and I don't know what he meant by "giving her some fool," but it sounded dirty to me!

KING (*sighing*): Why, don't you see that Lawrence was flattering your sweetheart? "Yankee" is an adjective from the Scottish lowlands, meaning a smart, forward woman. And my dear villain Longhair simply wanted to give her a dish of crushed fruit, which I believe your century calls "trifle." But, what's the use? Our centuries will never be able to understand each other.

It's true that words change their meaning over a period of time—sometimes so radically that the word means the opposite of what it meant originally. However, such changes come slowly, and it is rare for a word to change meaning completely within a generation.[4] The important thing in using words is to remember that their functions are (a) to name, (b) to assert, (c) to limit or measure, and (d) to connect. To achieve understanding, fine distinctions in meaning and subtle nuances of emotion, we must depend upon psychological factors *in addition to* words. In other words, we try to listen for what the person *means*, rather than to what he *says*.

During World War II, I was a Navy pilot. After returning from combat overseas, I was assigned to an aviation psychology division. They were trying to devise a test to predetermine whether or not an aviator would be effective in combat. The psychologists questioned hundreds and hundreds of fliers who had combat experience; each was asked to name (a) five fliers with whom he would *most* like to fly in combat, and give reasons why, and (b) five fliers with whom he would *not* like to fly in

---

[4] English is the richest of all languages in its vocabulary; instead of the conservative estimate of 750,000 words which I accept, some scholars claim as many as 5,000,000 words for the language! We add from 300 to 400 words each year (mostly technological ones) and find that about that same number have become obsolete in a year's time.

combat, and give reasons why. (All responses were strictly confidential.) My task was to take the responses from the pilots questioned and assign each response into one of thirty categories which the psychologists had set up. Very often, a flier's response would not fit into *any* of the categories set up by the psychologists, and I would go to my superior for directions.

"Why, he says 'So-and-so,'" the commander would reply, "so, that response goes under number fifteen."

"But that's not what he *means!*" I would protest. "What he actually means is . . ."

"Nevertheless, that's what he *says*, so that response goes under category fifteen," the commander would reply curtly, and so I put the response under number fifteen.

Although none of the psychologists working on the project had been trained as aviators and none of them had been near combat except when they visited a combat zone to question fliers, they boldly brushed aside the understanding of someone who had been trained as an aviator and who had combat experience! Instead, they relied entirely on what *they*—with completely different backgrounds—*thought* the aviators meant! In other words, they completely disregarded *meaning* and relied solely on *words*. It was a silly and useless project, and I got transferred away from it at the first opportunity.[5]

Jargon

It's hardly necessary to mention the fact that a layman, talking with a person from another occupation, must be particularly careful that he understands the special meanings that words and phrases take on in that occupation. In an office, a "traffic man-

[5] The responses of the combat fliers were fascinating from a human-relations point of view. For the most part, the reasons they gave for not wanting to fly combat with some pilot they named had nothing whatsoever to do with that man's courage or his ability to handle an airplane; instead, they picked out personality traits such as his being a poor loser at cards, his not doing his share of work in keeping the bunkroom clean, or his constantly borrowing money from other members of the squadron, and so on.

ager" does not direct automobiles; he only routes the mail and memoranda. In electronic computer circles, a "programmer" has nothing to do with entertainment; he sets up the computer to perform certain functions. And when a doctor feels around the upper part of a woman's chest, looking for a "thrill," there's nothing salacious about his action; he's looking for a vibration that indicates a special sort of heart condition.

> "Kill the baby!" the stagehand yells, and I shiver and shake with fright
> At the prospect of murder, but all that occurs is that someone puts out a light.
> "Burn one!" calls the restaurant counterman, and I picture a blackened steak,
> But the soda-jerk calmly empties a spoonful of malt in a "shake."
> The printer yells "Thirty!" and "Put her to bed!" and I wonder who's in distress;
> Thirty drinks? No wonder she's sleepy! But he simply means "Start up the press."
> The bartender calls "Eighty-six!" Is he giving a baseball score?
> Oh, no; he's telling the bouncer to toss some bum out the door.
> Oh, the strange and wonderful meanings in the world of jargonese
> Are a mystery to a layman. Won't someone "up-date me," please?

Obvious Psychological Pitfalls

In growing up and forming opinions about almost everything, we are proud of the fact that we have learned to pass judgment on most things around us, and we don't subscribe to outmoded beliefs such as the following:

> "A woman that's got a dimple in her chin
> Is almost always pushed by devils from within!"

> "People whose hair has turned gray early
> Are sure to have ways that are honest and pearly."

If we did accept these ideas, you can see in what conflict we would find ourselves if we encountered a woman with a dimpled chin *and* prematurely gray hair. Nevertheless, in the very process of learning to form opinions, we are apt to fall into habits that may block our understanding of others when talking with them.

Hasty conclusions

Toward the end of World War II, crowded conditions in New York City made it virtually impossible to find a vacant apartment. My friend Hal, who had made a great deal of money from the sale of a movie scenario, finally settled on a two-story "walk-up" in the midst of one of New York's worst slum areas. He had carpenters, plumbers and decorators come in and transform the vast loft into a luxurious apartment: lush, wall-to-wall carpeting, crystal chandeliers, pier mirrors, satin-tufted bedroom walls. Truly, it looked like a sumptuous movie setting! Hal and his brother, who was a medical student at Columbia, lived there; their sister, who was a registered private nurse, occasionally stayed overnight with them if she had a patient in the city.

One weekend, the medical student brought home from the zoology laboratory a large jar containing a pig embryo in formaldehyde; his home work was to dissect the embryo and make sketches for a report on it. Both Hal and his sister refused to allow the jar of formaldehyde in the refrigerator for preservation, so it was set out on the fire-escape in the winter weather. Early the next morning, Hal's sister arose, donned her nurse's uniform and was making coffee before leaving to go on duty. Suddenly there was a pounding on the door, accompanied by "Open up! It's the police!" It took Hal, his brother and his sister almost an hour to talk the policemen out of hauling the three of them down to the police station to be charged with running an abortion mill!

The evidence was certainly there: the neighbors in the surrounding tenements had long been puzzled by the glimpses of sybaritic splendor set amid the desolation of their own poor dwellings; they had become suspicious of the fact that Hal never seemed to go to work (he wrote at home), and that a woman in a nurse's uniform occasionally came and went; the embryo in the jar on the fire-escape was irrefutable "proof" that some dangerous hanky-panky was going on under their very noses. The policemen, too, had all the circumstantial evidence *they* needed: Why all this luxury in a slum district unless the abortionist was growing wealthy on fees collected from those who could not afford more children? Why the medical books strewn all over the place? Why the nurse? It seemed an airtight case, but both the neighbors and the police jumped to a false conclusion.

Consider another case from life:

I stepped into an already-packed elevator on one of the upper floors of a Chattanooga, Tennessee, hotel. We had descended perhaps three floors when a stout lady to my left swung around and slapped the face of a man standing behind her, at the same time commanding, "Stop this elevator and let me off—this minute!" The elevator operator obeyed and let her off at the next floor.

Everyone in the car was puzzled—especially the man who had been slapped. "What happened?" "What did you do to her?" "Why did she do that?" we asked the stricken passenger.

"I didn't do anything to her; never saw her before in my life!" he protested, rubbing his smarting face. Most of us shook our heads in disbelief. The elevator man kept the elevator at a standstill, pondering the mystery. Then: "I bit her!" said a small, frightened voice. It came from a diminutive lad of about five or six, who was backed into the corner alongside the man who had been slapped. "She was mashing me against the wall and I couldn't breathe, so I *bit* her!" The outraged lady had jumped to the conclusion that she was being "pinched" by the innocent man she had slapped!

People have suffered consequences much more serious than a slapped face because someone jumped to a hasty conclusion. Adult thinking *demands* that we think conclusively, but before jumping to a conclusion, or making a hasty generalization, let's ask ourselves a few questions:

1. Do we have sufficient evidence to come to a conclusion?

2. Is the source of our evidence reliable?

3. Could the evidence be mere coincidence, or has it existed over a sufficient period of time to be conclusive?

4. Is the conclusion that we draw a probable one, based on our life experience?

Closed minds

However probable a conclusion may seem, however much information you may have on any subject, you must not be deluded by the fact that you have *all* the information, or that the last word has been said on the subject. When Newton phrased his law of gravity, many people no doubt thought the final word on the subject was, "Everything that goes up must come down," but consider our space-age accomplishments of weightlessness and orbital objects that have defied gravity. You may recall that, many years ago, scientists "proved, beyond the shadow of a doubt," that the human body could not withstand speeds of more than thirty miles per hour; today, with men hurtling through space at 17,000 miles per hour, the last word probably still has not been said. You, as a business man or woman, must make decisions daily based on what sparse evidence is available, and there's nothing wrong with doing so. However, you should keep an open mind, and guard against slipping into the attitude of "My mind is made up; now, don't confuse me with more facts!"

POLICE LINE-UP

6½ FT
6 FT
5½ FT
5 FT
4½ F
4

Look at the drawing above for *no more than* ten seconds;
then try to answer the questions at the end of this chapter.

Subtle Psychological Skills

Have you ever listened to a conversation among three people
wherein each seemed to feel obligated to talk "to be sociable,"
but wherein no one made any real contact with anyone else? It
could have sounded like this:

STOCK-THINKER: I see in the paper that Pumpko and Philbitt
are planning a merger.

GIRL-THINKER: Oh? I hadn't heard. By the way, Gus Monck
married that chorus girl he was dating.

TERMITE-THINKER: Yes! Surprised everybody. They're living in
my neighborhood. Hope they don't have as much trouble with
termites as I've had.

STOCK-THINKER: I've got a few shares of Pumpko stock, you know. Don't know whether the merger will water it down or increase its value. What do you think?

TERMITE-THINKER: It all depends. There ought to be a law against selling houses with termites. Cost me a fortune to get rid of them.

GIRL-THINKER: I just can't see a "square" like old Gus married to a high-stepper. Do you suppose it will last?

STOCK-THINKER: Well, last time I owned stock in a merger, it split three ways and jumped five dollars per share. Five dollars overnight! Maybe she'll do it again.

GIRL-THINKER: I'll bet when all of Gus's woman-chasing bachelor friends learn that he's married Cillie Sans Rien, he'll have a house full of guests every weekend. It'll cost him a fortune!

TERMITE-THINKER: Yep, it costs a fortune to get rid of 'em.

STOCK-THINKER: Not if she sells at a five-dollar per share gain. He'll make a million!

Now, they're thinking together—or, does it only *sound* like it? One of our basic failures in communicating with others and understanding others is this lack of contact. It literally amounts to talking with one's self, and is responsible for many a hurt in both business and social life. This isolationism can be avoided if you will practice these things: Recognize the motivation, purpose and urgency behind another's speech, and the frame of reference from which that speech is made.

Recognizing purpose or objective

The scene is a dog kennel, where there are several varieties of dogs for sale. I approach the owner, who is wandering among the dog-pens, filling the watering pans.

I: I'd like to buy a dog.

K: Well, they're all for sale. What kind did you have in mind?

I: Personally, I've always admired a Doberman pinscher. I think my wife would like one, also, because of its short hair.

ᴋ: Well, there are two sharp Doberman pups over there. One is six months old and the other is three.

ɪ: Yes, they're both beauties! What's the price on them?

ᴋ: The older one is $125, and the younger one $100.

ɪ: Oh, I think I'd prefer the younger one, so I can train him just as I like. (I'll also save myself $25.00.)

[*I return two weeks later.*]

ɪ (*angrily*): Look here, you didn't play quite fair and square with me about that dog I bought. The dog got sick, I had to take him to the veterinarian, who said he needed all sorts of shots. Cost me thirty dollars.

ᴋ: You didn't ask me. Now, the older puppy had already *had* all those inoculations; that's why he was $25 higher.

ɪ: Well, of all the nerve!

[*I return after a month, angrier than before.*]

ɪ: Do you make it a habit to mislead all your customers? That damned dog you sold me is a positive menace to my little four- and six-year-old boys; snarls at them, won't play with them; won't have anything to do with anybody but my wife. Most anti-social animal I've ever seen!

ᴋ: Yep, Dobermans are one-person dogs. Not much good for young children. Boxers, cockers, dachshunds—even poodles—are better with youngsters.

ɪ: Why didn't you tell me?

ᴋ: You said you liked a Doberman, and that your wife wanted a shorthaired dog. You didn't tell me you wanted a dog for your children.

In this example, both parties are at fault: I, for not making my purpose clearer, and the kennel owner for not trying to ascertain my objective in buying a dog. In the next case, the person fails to get the clue to my motivation even though I state it plainly.

I am talking with a friend who has traveled widely:

"I have a week's vacation with extra pay, and the wife and I would like to get away for a quiet rest. We don't particularly care about the seashore, but we do want a place where there's warm sunshine. Any suggestions?"

"Of course!" he replies enthusiastically. "The only place for you to go is to the Riviera Hotel in Las Vegas. Rooms are about thirty feet long, air-conditioned, and positively soundproof. The desert sun is marvelous. And there's something going on all around the clock. You can go from one lounge show to another all up and down The Strip; entertainment goes on until five in the morning. If you don't like to play the slot machines, you can play roulette, blackjack, craps or almost any game you like. I'm telling you, there is so much to do and see that you need a *month* there! I only stayed four days my last trip, and I didn't get three hours sleep any night, there were so many exciting things to do. There's a dinner show and a midnight show at all the big hotels; it's really the entertainment capital of the world. Go to Las Vegas!"

Evaluating urgency

"Grown people never listen to what children say," a nine-year-old boy once confided; "grownups decide what they're going to answer the minute we start talking." That unfortunate break in communication is not confined to adult-child relationships. Too often in talking with one another, we fail to recognize the urgency in another's need. If I stop a friend on the street and say to him, "You've seen this movie. It's going to start in five minutes, and I can't decide whether or not to see it; is it a good movie?" and he launches into a fifteen-minute, detailed description of the movie's plot, he has obviously ignored the urgency in my request. However, we ignore urgency in the voice of others in the same way. A rapid rate of speech, a sudden huskiness or break in the voice, an inordinately high pitch—all may indicate some definite need for recognition of one sort or urgency or another, and if we are to understand others, we must recognize their needs.

Once, I took a summer job directing motor-coach tours of Canada. My bus driver was a big, happy-go-lucky Irishman with a fine sense of humor, but with a temper that flared up like lighted gasoline. One day we pulled up and stopped alongside an automobile at a railroad crossing to wait for a passing train. There was a thundering crash and everyone in our bus was jolted forward; some vehicle had crashed into our rear. His face red with anger, my driver opened the bus door and bolted out, determined to punch in the nose the careless driver who had ploughed into us. From the offending vehicle—which was a dilapidated pick-up truck with most of its body missing—emerged an elderly, skinny man in overalls, grinning from ear to ear. He spoke before my driver could shout at him.

"Shore do thank you, Son! Shore do! I ain't got a sign of a brake on that thing and I had to hit somethin' to keep from runnin' into that train, so I picked on you 'cause you was the biggest!"

My driver, recognizing the old hayseed's urgency, stopped in his tracks and hooted with laughter.

Frames of reference

Whatever we think, whatever we hear, whatever we say—all depend upon our life experience as a whole. Some attitudes which we have spent years developing cannot be changed overnight; others, about which we do not feel so strongly, may be changed by a single dramatic happening. If we recognize that this is true of everyone, it will help avoid misunderstanding when talking with others. The following mental exercise may be far-fetched—may even seem a little absurd to you—but it carries a very valuable lesson in communicating with others:

You are walking alongside a stream of water and you hear a tiny voice say, "I am a fish. I have never seen a man, but I have heard men talk. Tell me, please: What are shoes?" Try to put into words what you would say to the fish to make him understand what shoes are. (You cannot say simply, "They are coverings for one's feet," for if he has never seen a man he would not know what feet are.)

Obviously, if you are to make the fish understand what shoes are, you must talk to him in terms of what he already knows—you must literally "enter the world of the fish." You might compare man's legs and feet to the fish's pectoral fins; you might compare man's need for foot-covering to the fish's need for scales on his body, and so on. The chances are that you might not be able to give the fish an exact picture of what shoes *look* like without going into tedious details (also from his world), but he would have a pretty good idea of their function, and that idea would be meaningful to him because you considered his *frame of reference*. For an American to talk about personal freedom with a Russian who has been born and brought up in Communist Russia, with no access to outside literature, pictures, and ideas, is foolish and futile; "personal freedom" means an entirely different thing in the Russian's frame of reference.

Individual needs in one's frame of reference

Fifteen years ago a clinical psychologist told me that a person in our present-day civilization needs satisfaction in four areas to be emotionally stable. She said that satisfaction could be lacking in one of those areas, if that lack was compensated by especially strong satisfaction in the three other areas; that it might be possible for a person to lack satisfaction in *two* areas, provided *extreme* satisfaction was provided in the two remaining areas; but, that if a person lacked satisfaction in three of the four areas, he would be in grave trouble emotionally. Since I was told this, I have observed intimate friends and close acquaintances (whose needs I was aware of) in their relationships with others, and my clinical psychologist's observation has proved dramatically true. In considering a person's frame of reference, you should ask yourself how satisfied that person is (and how satisfied *you* are) in these four areas:

1. *Emotional satisfaction.* It's hard to judge this; who can say whether the man who lives with the girl of his dreams and their five harassing children in a trim bungalow, mortgaged up to the hilt, from whence he commutes to a drudging job each morning and returns each evening to a nightmare of lawns to be trimmed and storm windows to be removed, is happier than the lonely spinster "career girl," who lives in a city apartment with only a tiny poodle on which to lavish her affection? However, I think we may make a safe generalization about this need by saying that most people want to be loved, or want something *to* love. This need is depicted in a tragic and beautiful way by John Steinbeck in his novel *Of Mice and Men,* wherein George, the quick-witted farm laborer, needs Lennie, his half-witted brute companion, quite as much as Lennie needs George. Apparently, everyone wants to be needed by some living thing, or person, in some way.

2. *Accomplishment satisfaction.* This is the creative urge, dealt with in a subsequent chapter. It doesn't matter much whether what one creates is *good* or not; the fact that he has created it is enough. Industrial psychologists tell me that when a man employed to do a routine or "assembly-line" job starts giving trouble, one of the first things they try to learn is what he does in his spare time. If he stops each day at the neighborhood bar, has a few beers with the same cronies, goes home and has dinner, then sits down to watch television until bedtime, they're worried. However, if he says that he grows dahlias, sculptures soap, does creative cooking or builds cabinets, they feel that his personal problems in the shop have a better chance of being solved. The widespread fad of "do-it-yourself" in America is no doubt motivated by the unconscious desire to do something creative to satisfy this need.

Because of this desire for accomplishment, we have allowed such things as food, clothing and shelter to become status symbols of our ability to create or accomplish. We do not want clothes to cover our nakedness—we want *fine* clothes; we do not want mere shelter from the elements—we want a house that is bigger than that of the Blodgetts' next door; and we are not content with food for physical nourishment—we want to dine at the Forum of the Twelve Caesars!

3. *Recognition satisfaction.* It is not enough that we accomplish or create something; we want recognition for doing so. This need is apt to be felt keenly by those who do a routine or "assembly-line" job. Too often a supervisor is deluded by the fact that all is going smoothly and efficiently in the office or in the shop. He does not realize that, out of sheer boredom, a worker may deliberately sabotage work operations or human relations. An occasional word of praise about the worker's keeping production up, or his cheerfulness on the job, or even a sincere compliment on the worker's appearance, may be insurance against an emotional outburst later on.

I directed professional summer theatre for several seasons. During the first summer, the young leading woman was one whose talents and personality I admired tremendously. I was therefore surprised when she approached me at a party halfway through the summer and greeted me with,

"I've wanted to ask you all summer long, why don't you like me?"

"My dear Colleen, I adore you!"

"But you don't think I'm a very good actress, do you?"

"I not only think that you're a good actress, but I honestly believe that within a few years you will be one of America's greatest actresses." (And she was, incidentally.)

"Then why haven't you once said a good word about my work during rehearsal, when you've praised every bit player and every apprentice who has appeared on stage?" she asked.

I was dumfounded. I had always praised her performance on opening night. At rehearsal I had thought that she knew that her work was so fine that I never *needed* to give her much direction, whereas I had to sweat out performances with some of the lesser actors. After practically bludgeoning them, I always praised them when they came through in a halfway decent manner; yet I almost wrecked the morale of the company by neglecting recognition of *her* work *in rehearsal*.

4. *Group membership satisfaction.* The old saying that man is a gregarious animal is still true. He needs to belong to some group. Just after World War II hundreds of thousands of veterans were beset by emotional difficulties, many of them attributable to a sense of no longer "belonging" anywhere. A young man would return to his neighborhood to discover that the social group to which he had belonged had dissolved; he would go down to the office and re-claim his job, only to find the place filled with strangers who spoke nothing in common with him; even his church group had taken on an unfamiliar aspect. Since he was deprived of the camaraderie of his military outfit, he no longer felt he belonged *anywhere*. What he did not realize was that, in civilian life, he had *grown* into groups gradually; in military life he was *thrown* into a group and had to make the best of it, and that, returning to civilian life, he would once again have to *grow* into other groups gradually. Groups do not usually accept an outsider instantly, nor does an outsider feel at ease instantly within a new group. Most people do have this need, however, and in considering a person's frame of reference one must consider the groups to which he belongs—or the groups to which he would *like* to belong.

Cliques

While on the subject of people belonging to groups, we should consider the *cliques* which people form. A *clique* differs from a formal organization in that it has no specific set of by-laws and no openly elected officers; it is simply a group of people who band together for various reasons, and who tend to support one another's opinions. But, while a *clique* has no elected officers, it definitely does have a leader or two who exert a strong influence over the others. Business executives take a dim view of *cliques* within their firms—an attitude that is wholly unrealistic. When the same people work together day after day, they are inevitably going to gravitate toward other personalities who attract them—groups smaller and more comfortable than the large corporation. Personnel directors and other business executives should accept this inevitability and—instead of fearing it—learn how to handle it.

A recent article in a business magazine suggested that the business executive handle *cliques* by joining them, thereby getting each *clique* to work for the company's best interests. This is sheer nonsense. No man can be all things to all men, and to attempt to horn your way into each group which has its own common interests could engender jealousy among various groups, produce resentment in groups who do not wish to accept you, earn you the reputation of being a "buttinsky," and lower the respect of your subordinates. However, here are a few suggestions for dealing with *cliques:*

First, try to understand what the common interests are within a *clique;* it may be something as innocuous as the fact that they attend the same bowling alley on a Thursday night. Second, try to locate the leader and consider his own personal frame of reference; you can deal with the *clique* as a whole by understanding its leader and earning his respect. Third, show no partiality for any one group, however much you yourself may have in common with that particular group. Lastly, try not to resent the fact that workers select their own social leader, who often is *not* their supervisor on the job. *Cliques* are not necessarily an undermining factor in a business. They can be the means of lifting morale by giving a worker an added sense of belongingness.

In closing this chapter, let me say that it is not necessary to psychoanalyze a person in order to communicate well with him. It is necessary to realize the limitations of words, to try to understand how your words will be received by others who have a different frame of reference, and to consider personal differences when one is listening to another. Remember, we selfishly seek for those who appear sympathetic to us, but we hesitate to extend our understanding to others who may not have our own comfortable "frame of reference."

"Police Line-Up" drawing on *page 34*: Without turning back to the drawing, how many of these questions can you answer?

1. Which man in the group is the tallest? The shortest?
2. Which man is holding a fan? A knife? A hat?
3. Look again at the drawing. Did you jump to any hasty conclusions in your answers?

Chapter Two

Are You Listening?

TWO friends stood to the right of me in a quiet San Francisco bar. A man stepped up to the bar on my left and said in a loud, clear voice, "Bourbon and soda, please."

"Scotch and soda? Yes sir!" the bartender responded, reaching for the Scotch.

"No, I said bourbon and soda."

"Sorry, sir. Any particular brand?"

I turned to my companion furthest away from the stranger. "Did you hear that man order his drink the first time?" I asked.

"Sure. He asked for bourbon and soda. The bartender just wasn't paying attention."

Now, the bartender was looking directly at the stranger when he spoke, and was directly across the bar from him, while my friend was three bodies away. Perhaps the barkeep thought the stranger *looked* like a Scotch drinker, so he heard what he *expected* to hear. Or, perhaps he wasn't listening. It was a trivial matter, but the same thing happens all the time in more serious matters.

Up until a few years ago, little or no attention was given to the *skill* of listening. People either paid attention to you or they didn't. However, during World War II, we discovered that one of the primary causes of combat fatigue in aviators was the strain caused by trying to hear and be heard on interplane radios against a noise background, and so we conducted a number of studies and experiments on speech intelligibility and on listening ability. One of the most rewarding results of those studies and experiments was the discovery that the listening ability of a person can be improved. (This is quite apart from his hearing acuity.) This chapter will give a few suggestions on how you can improve your listening ability and perhaps your ability to retain what you *listen to*—as distinguished from what you hear.

Concentration

One of the first things you must recognize if you want to improve your listening skill is that it requires physical energy and concentration to listen well. Once I took a position which offered me the opportunity to coach pupils privately for extra money in my spare time, and I took on about twenty in addition to my regular classes. At the end of the term I was puzzled by my fatigue. I cut down on the number of private pupils the following term and found that my fatigue lessened. I was puzzled. It was more tiring to sit in my comfortable apartment and teach a private pupil than it was to teach a classroom full of people. I mentioned this to a colleague who had more than thirty years of experience in the field of speech. She remarked, "I'm surprised that you haven't discovered this before. When you're teaching a class, you draw from past experience and your general store of information, but when you're teaching a private pupil you concentrate on *listening*, which is the hardest work I know of, if you are conscientious about it." If you wish to improve your listening skill, you must recognize the fact that listening is an active—not a passive—act, and that it does require concentration.

Divided attention

You cannot listen well to more than one thing at a time. In my classes in voice and diction and foreign accent correction, I ask my students to promise, during the time they are taking the course, not to turn on their radio or television sets unless they are sitting down and giving *full* attention to what they are hearing. The deplorable habit of Americans having background music for everything they do can actually cripple the mental, emotional and creative abilities of a person, according to Dr. Franz Winkler.[1] Officials of a plush New York department store experimented on canned music in its store to relieve the monotony of work for their retail clerks. They discovered that if they suffused their store with soft music for a period of fifteen minutes at about 11 A.M. and again at about 3:30 P.M., the efficiency and job-attitude of the clerks improved. They increased the music broadcasts to a half hour and noted that there was no further improvement. Then, they increased the broadcast period to an hour twice daily and noticed that there was a definite *drop* in their clerks' efficiency and job-attitude.[2] When the music was broadcast for the entire day, the store not only got many reports of inefficiency, but overt complaints from clerks and customers alike that they couldn't keep their minds on buying and selling. The diversion that the short fifteen minutes of music brought at the height of the fatigue periods was welcome, but a constant division of attention acted as an irritant.

[1] "Beware of Background Music," *This Week Magazine,* Sept. 17, 1961, p. 17.
[2] Determined from a free-response questioning generally about "How do you like your job?"

Distractions

One of the reasons that we don't remember the names of people to whom we're introduced is that we're so busy looking them over we don't concentrate on their names. When we're called into the boss' office for instructions we must beware of distractions such as "Gee! It's warm in here," "The boss has a new picture of his family on his desk," "I hope this isn't going to take too long; I've asked that new secretary to take her coffee break with me." For many summers I took a job as a tourist guide. One of the first things I was taught was to let my tourists look for a moment at a new sight before trying to explain it to them; otherwise, they would not grasp the explanation.

Practice

It may seem foolish to you, but you can actually increase your listening skill by doing a very simple thing. Each day, close your eyes for one minute and concentrate on the sounds you hear about you. Try it in different places where you find yourself. Don't think of anything except what you can *hear*. In this noisy age, we learn to shut out sounds for our own comfort; we do this unconsciously and it becomes a habit. This habit can be detrimental when we really want to listen to something, so we need to be able to break the habit at will. Try it! Incidentally, we also tend to shut out sights that do not concern us at the moment. Once I asked a freshman composition class in New York City to report on what they saw on the second and third stories of the buildings in the block where they lived, and they were surprised at what they had been missing in life by not "looking up."

If you can get a friend to work with you (you and your spouse may enjoy this as a parlor game, preferable to watching some inane television program), you can train yourself to listen by practising following directions involving several details. Here are some samples, but you yourself should be able to invent more; they should be *heard*, not looked at:

1. Draw a square and place in it the letter "i" with a dot above it. (There should be *two* dots above the vertical line.)

2. You are a city bus driver. You have fourteen passengers aboard when you reach Lexington Avenue; there you discharge three passengers and take on two; at your next stop you take on seven more passengers; at Missouri Avenue four passengers get off, and two get on; and at Detroit Avenue eight passengers get off to take the subway. You take on three passengers at both Eighth and Ninth Avenues. By the time you reach Tenth Avenue can you answer the following questions?

a. What is the bus driver's name?
b. How many times have you stopped?
c. Which came first, Missouri or Detroit Avenue?

(Who cares how many passengers you have left at this point?)

3. Go to storage locker No. 474 and open it. You will find there 47 boxes of paper clips and 77 boxes of rubber bands. Bring me 17 boxes of paper clips and 24 boxes of rubber bands. On your way back here, stop off and pick up 77 four-cent stamps. Was the number of the storage locker 477, 744, 474 or 747?

4. This crooked line represents the Snake River. The "X" in the middle of the river marks the spot where an airliner crashed and killed 47 people. On which side of the river will you bury the survivors? (One doesn't bury survivors—but who listens to such details?)

"Black-out" areas

"My mind went completely blank" is a common expression. When we hear it we assume it to be a hyperbole and think little of it. However, it occurs more often than we realize to people who are *not* intoxicated—and results in serious misunderstandings. For each of us there are certain words, phrases or ideas that have such unpleasant associations or connotations that we literally stop listening when we hear someone use them. The word need not be an emotion-laden one, nor the phrase suggest an unpleasant event; it may be a word as innocent as "Hello." I knew a woman for whom that simple word had such an unpleasant association that she forbade her children to use it as a greeting!

The insidious property of these "black-out" areas is that we may not be aware of them. Nevertheless, let someone use one of these "bad" words and we stop listening and start thinking: (a) That person is my enemy, he does not like the same things I like; (b) I must refute him, or conquer him in some way; (c) when I have succeeded in showing him that I am superior, what will his reaction be? You can see that if the thoughts expressed in the foregoing sentence occupy your mind, you cannot be listening to what the other person is saying.

There are words whose unpleasant connotations and associations are obvious: Spic, nigger, kike, swamp angel, sex pervert, leprosy, whore, child-molester, bigot, bastard, scabies, hoodlum, contraceptive, and so forth. However, here are examples of three perfectly innocent words which blocked listening ability for three of my adult students. I admit they are extreme examples, but I assure you that these people were educated, mature business men and women.

1. *Chicken.* A mother of college graduates not only refused to eat chicken, but would actually break out in goose pimples when the word was mentioned. Discussing the word with an older sister revealed that my student had been given a pet baby chick and that the family had eaten the chicken when it was grown.

2. *Litter.* A lawyer was so offended by this word that he deplored the street signs put up by the city advising people not to be "litterbugs." "Litter" was the term used by his nurse for faeces during his toilet-training stage.

3. *Dawn.* Poetry or prose was spoiled for a proof-reader when it contained this word. One day his mother chanced to mention that an aunt who had once lived with them prefaced almost everything she said with, "It just dawned on me." This aunt had looked after my student for the first three years of his life while his mother worked, had later been committed to an insane asylum and was never seen again by him.

What can we do to prevent these "black-out" areas from spoiling our listening ability? The first thing to do is to identify them. The next time you hear a person use a word that you dislike, make a mental note of it. Write it down if possible. The next time someone brings up a subject that is embarrassing or unpleasant for you to discuss, make a note of that also. Then, discuss the matter with a friend in whom you have the utmost confidence. You don't need to consult a psychiatrist, a clergyman or even a college professor, because the unpleasant association is in your own mind and talking about it—bringing it to a conscious level—will often reveal the cause of your dislike. The friend with an aversion to the word "hello" discovered that she associated it with a relative who frequently punished her unjustly when she was a child and who always greeted people with an over-cheerful, expansive "Hello!" Even if you are unable to find the reason why you dislike certain words, phrases or ideas, the fact that you have identified them will help you; you can be on guard when you hear one of them, and determine not to let that puny word block your listening. After all, adults should be able to discuss anything that exists without becoming emotionally upset.

Structure and meaning

Have you ever told someone a story and found that he "missed the point" completely? It's an experience common to all of us. Most of you have heard the anecdote of the husband who asked his wife,

"Have you heard the story about the dirty window?"

"No, what is it?"

"Oh, well, you couldn't see through it anyway."

The next day the wife thought she would repeat this to a neighbor, so she asked,

"Have you heard the story about the window you couldn't see through?"

"No," replied the neighbor; "how does it go?"

"Oh, well, it's too dirty to tell anyway."

Experts in communication estimate that only about *one fourth* of all adult listeners are able to get the main idea when listening to a speaker. Small wonder that the average industrial firm spends upwards of $35,000 a year on salaries for the time spent in meetings and conferences among their management staff members! Sometimes this failure to understand what a speaker really *means* is the fault of the speaker; he has failed to organize his thoughts so that the main idea can be recognized. Often, however, we listeners fail to get the main idea because we become absorbed with a minor part of a communication. Read aloud the passage below and ask a listener to give you the central idea.

Religious men have not always followed the tenets of brotherly love advocated in the New Testament. Indeed, they have used their religion as an excuse to commit some of the most atrocious acts known to mankind. Witness the Spanish Inquisition, during which an estimated 30,000 people were executed in the name of religion. Between the 11th and 18th centuries, when separation of church and state was nebulous, almost 9,000,000 people were put to death for practising witchcraft. The carefree Polynesian race, as innocently naked as Adam and Eve in the Garden of Eden, almost became extinct because the Protestant missionaries insisted on clothing them, but did not warn them that they would fall prey to pneumonia and tuberculosis if they did not remove their wet clothing after swimming. There are other instances, too numerous to mention, where men have used their religious beliefs as an excuse to uphold their prejudices and selfish interests at the expense of torture and death to other men.

Reading this aloud to a group of adults, I have received such varied responses as "The writer is anti-Catholic," "The writer is anti-Protestant," "The writer is an atheist," and "The writer believes in nudism." Did you or your listener get the central idea? It was expressed twice in that brief paragraph.

One should learn to listen for *structure* as well as for the main idea. You should know the basic structures which writers and speakers are likely to use, and try to identify the one being used by the speaker you are listening to. This will not only help you understand what he means, but it will also help you retain what you have heard. Above all, try to distinguish between a main point and supporting material; don't let the tail wag the dog.

Transitional points

One of the most valuable aids to listening—and to retention —is the practice of reviewing quickly what a speaker has already said as he moves from one topic to another. "How can I be reviewing what he *has said,* when I'm supposed to be listening to what he *is saying?*" This is simple enough to do because of the difference in the speeds of thought and speech. We think at about four times the speed at which we speak. So, when a speaker reaches a transitional point in his talking, it is fairly easy to ask yourself, "What has he said so far?" and summarize for yourself. This is made easier for you if you are listening to a skillful speaker, for he will always use material to support each point he makes—sometimes two or three kinds of supportive material—and you need only remember the main point. A good speaker will also make his transitions clear, which gives you a little more time in which to recapitulate what he has already said.

If you use a little self-discipline and practise listening actively, if you listen to what a person means instead of what you may have presupposed he was going to mean, if you distinguish between his main points and subsidiary material, and if you review his ideas at transitional points, you will find that your understanding of others will improve and your own knowledge will increase.

Chapter Three

The Information Comes Through

ABOUT three-fourths of all our waking hours is spent in some form of communication. A breakdown of that time is shown in the illustration.

You can see that the majority of that communication time is spent in listening and talking. (The proportion of talking and listening may vary, according to whether you're a man or woman.) Listening and talking about *what?* Over a long period of years I have asked many business and professional people what kind of listening and talking occupies most of their time; their responses were overwhelmingly in favor of *giving and getting information.* Even among salesmen, persuading other people ranked second to this important activity of acquiring and passing on information of one sort or another. It forms a great part of even our social conversation. Yet, the fact that most of us arc unskilled in this important speaking activity is shown by the frequency with which we hear the following statements (usually spoken in indignation or consternation):

"I explained it so clearly that even an idiot should have understood!"

"But I didn't understand a word you said!"

"You just didn't listen to what I was telling you!"

"You misinformed me grossly; nobody could be expected to read *your* mind—not even if he could read the Lord's Prayer printed on a pin-head!"

"You're a blockhead!"

"And you can't think straight—nor talk straight!"

You spend about 75% of your waking hours in some form of communication.

How can such recriminations be avoided? They *can* be, if each of us will recognize that giving and getting information involves skills that must be learned—skills that do not come automatically because you've learned to repeat back-fence gossip or tell a funny story in the locker room at the country club. First, let's talk about the skills involved in *giving* information.

Preparing to Give Information

First of all, you must organize your information.

"Of course," you say, "everybody knows that!" Then, having paid lip service to organization, you jot down a few notes and rush pell-mell into giving your listener a hodgepodge of information without unity, coherence or emphasis. Here are a few pointers in organizing information to be given orally:

1. Give a broad over-view, a general purpose or a summary first, so that your listener will have an idea of what to expect.

> *Example:* Here are a few things that the head of a shipping department should know in order to help him work with salesmen in the field. There are three things which are expected of the head of the shipping department...
>
> *Example:* So that you may understand better our operation, let me show you how our expenditures are related to our sales. Perhaps the most striking thing is that the amount of money we spend in an area does not necessarily guarantee the highest sales. Take, for example...

2. Select only the main points, and arrange them in order of importance. Don't get lost in a plethora of tedious details; once you have given the listener the main points, details can be taken care of by questions and answers or—in the case of an operation—by on-the-spot instruction.

3. Try not to omit any important points, so that you will not have to resort to, "Oh, I forgot to tell you . . ."

4. Explain any jargon or technical terms as you use them. Don't assume that the listener knows as much as you do about the information you are going to give. Keep your language as simple as possible.

5. Use more than one medium, if possible. Words are tricky, as we have seen in a previous chapter; use drawings, diagrams, charts, but keep them simple and free of minor details. Examine Tables I and II, the results of a survey of three cities to determine who decides on what car the family buys. Table I is cluttered with useless information, while Table II gets at the desired information at a glance.

TABLE I

PERSONS IN HOUSEHOLD
WHO DECIDE WHAT FAMILY CAR TO BUY

Person in Household	*Northeastern City*	*Western City*	*Southern City*
Husband	31.0%	38.0%	14.7%
Wife	20.4	18.7	46.0
Husband and wife	47.0	42.0	37.0
Daughter or son	1.3	0.1	0.9
Wife and daughter	—	0.1	1.0
Husband and son	—	1.0	0.1
Wife and son	—	—	0.2
Husband and daughter	0.1	0.1	—
Mother-in-law	0.2	—	0.1
	100.0%	100.0%	100.0%

Table I might have been extended to include the influence which neighbors, servants and television advertising had on choosing the family car, but the percentages would be so small that they would only clutter up the table and make the *significant* figures difficult to find, which may be stated thus: "In the cities surveyed, the husband and wife together select the family

car; in cities where one or the other alone selects the car, it tends
to be the wife, particularly in the South." Notice, also, that in
Table II the highest percentages are listed first.

TABLE II

WHO DECIDES ON FAMILY CAR

Person	Northeastern City	Western City	Southern City
Husband and wife	47.0%	42.0%	37.0%
Wife	20.4	18.7	46.0
Husband	31.0	38.0	14.7
Others	1.5	1.3	2.3
	100.0%	100.0%	100.0%

If you can express your information graphically—using still
another medium—it is well to do so, in passing on information;
notice how the information from Table II is available at a glance
in Chart A.

WHO PICKS THE FAMILY CAR?

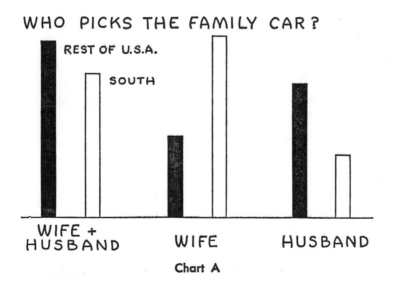

Chart A

A poster for relief of starving children in China may startle one by stating that 70,000 children will starve in that huge nation before the end of the year. A poster with *one picture* of a bright-eyed but emaciated Chinese youngster, captioned "70,000 of us will starve without your help!" will have far more effect on the viewer. He is even apt to recall the figures better.

Giving the Information

Use of several media

In the previous section, we hinted that the person giving information use more than one medium to express himself; there are three other media which you can use in the actual passing on of the information. They are (a) questions, (b) taking notes and (c) playbacks.

Encourage the person who is receiving the information to ask questions. To this end, you must be careful to go slowly enough for the receiver of your information to feel that he may interrupt to ask questions or take notes. If you appear in a hurry to get the information delivered and done with, the receiver will hesitate to ask questions or take notes, and both are valuable assets in insuring that information gets through intact. When you see the receiver start to take notes, wait until he has had a chance to finish his notes. At each transitional point, stop and encourage him to ask questions. In giving information, haste not only makes waste, but also misunderstanding.

If the information you are passing on is long and complicated, it is well to do a "re-cap" or summary at the end, preceding it with some statement such as, "Now, here are the three important things that you will need to remember..." (Try to have no more than three to five at the most.)

Perhaps the single most important device to be used in giving information effectively is the use of the "playback"; that is, asking the receiver of the information to repeat the information you have given. It utilizes another medium—the receiver's verbalizing the information on his own—and is an almost sure guarantee of the information's being preserved intact. Yet, this is one step that most business executives hesitate to take when giving information. Why? The following incident explains their proud—and shortsighted—reasoning.

I had just explained to a group of business men the importance of using the "playback" in giving information. One of them objected strongly to its use. I asked him to state his objections.

"I'm a busy man," he answered. "If I took the time to ask everyone I give information to to repeat that information, I'd never get my job done. Also, I'd insult the intelligence of every one of my subordinates by asking them to repeat information I'd given them. They're intelligent; they can understand English."

"Then, I take it, you never have any misunderstandings when you give information to any of your subordinates?" I suggested.

"All the time!" he exploded. "Some idiot is constantly misinterpreting what I tell him—but it's because he just doesn't *listen!*"

"Well, isn't a playback a pretty good way of finding out how well he has listened? Wouldn't it save a lot of time in unsnarling things later on?" I ventured.

But he only snorted, "Nonsense!"

There's no need for a request for a playback to embarrass either the party giving or the party receiving the information. If you're giving the information and feel that the person receiving it may be sensitive about his intelligence being underestimated, it's a simple matter to put your request in this manner: "Charley, I'm not sure that I've really covered all I intended to. Would you mind going over the data I've given you, and I'll think along as you're doing it to see if I've omitted anything you should know ... Thank you."

Permanent and temporary attitudes

In the chapter on "Understanding" we emphasized the importance of considering the frame of reference of the other person, and the fact that all of us have "deaf spots." These factors are important in preventing information from getting through intact to others, or in helping to get the information across. Psychologists say that all of us have permanent and temporary attitudes toward various things. The permanent attitude is that attitude which has developed over the years through our environment, the influence of family, friends and groups to which we belong; the temporary attitude is the attitude we take toward something because we're feeling out of sorts temporarily. (Perhaps the baby kept us awake all night, or we have a toothache, or the bus driver en route to work was particularly rude.) Our permanent attitudes are not apt to change except after years of re-education or under extreme pressure; our temporary attitudes may change within an hour or two. Both must be recognized and considered when faced with the problem of getting information across. Here are two case histories that illustrate each:

1. Mary Faber is an expert stenographer. She wants to work for Litchfield Mills, but they do not have an opening at present for a stenographer, although they expect one soon. So, Mary agrees to work temporarily as a file clerk and handler of accident reports. Because she has a quick mind, her filing is fast and accurate, often leaving much free time on her hands. On the other hand, the handling of accident reports is tedious, routine and time-consuming, and is no challenge to Mary's intelligence and training. She has learned yesterday that Miss Schnapps has postponed her wedding and will remain with the Litchfield Company indefinitely. Mary was supposed to step into Miss Schnapps' position as stenographer as soon as Miss Schnapps married and left the company. This morning Mary's supervisor brings her a stack of accident reports, and says brightly, "Mary, here is a stack

of accident reports that require a new method of processing; Corinne has not been able to get to them because she is behind on her filing. Will you sit down and let me explain the new process to you, please?"

Is the information on how to process the new type of accident report likely to get through to Mary? Hardly! Her permanent attitude has been: "I am too valuable to be wasted as a file clerk." Her temporary attitude is: "I am bitterly disappointed that Miss Schnapps has decided to stay on, so that I won't get the job promised me; and I resent having to do the work of that nincompoop Corinne just because she can't keep up with her own job."

2. Ray Kowalsky is production line manager in a firm that manufactures appliances. He is proud of his position and his output, since he had relatively little schooling and has come up the hard way. His supervisor, Tom Kent, is a graduate engineer, and has been ordered to put a new type of guard on certain lathes in Ray's assembly line. Tom would like to have the guards put on during working hours, to avoid overtime which maintenance men would charge if put on after closing time. He telephones Ray.

"Ray, we've been ordered to replace the guards on the lathes in your assembly line."

"That's what I hear."

"Now, I could have the maintenance men do the job tonight, but I'm opposed to that. I'd be charged for their time, and I've got so many charges for overtime already this month, that I thought we'd do it this afternoon about two o'clock, so . . ."

"What! And shut down operations? Nothin' doin'! I'm behind in my output now, and it ain't my fault that you can't manage without havin' men put in so much overtime."

And Ray slams down the receiver, plows into the office of the big boss and accuses Tom of trying to sabotage his production output. His permanent attitude was probably one of resentment of a "college whippersnapper" holding down a position superior to his own; his temporary attitude was that he was being penalized because of the inefficiency of that same "whippersnapper."

Either case could have been handled without—or, certainly, with less—friction, had the supervisors considered the probable attitudes of others. Mary's supervisor might have expressed her sympathy at what was obviously a disappointment on Mary's part, reassured her that the reason she was being kept on was that the Litchfield management considered her valuable and would find the right niche for her later, and appealed to her superior intelligence in learning the new procedure for accident reports. Tom Kent might have *asked* Ray Kowalsky *when* the new guards could be placed on the lathes so as to least interfere with Ray's production output.

Sometimes, it is difficult to determine the attitude of the person to whom you are passing on information, and you must be alert to clues the receiver may give in his comments, or in your previous knowledge about his religion, his membership in groups, and his initiative and ability to take and offer criticism.

Avoid unnecessary channels

Spoken information that is passed through as many as four persons will almost invariably be subject to (a) distortions or changes, (b) imaginings or additions, and (c) some omissions of vital portions. This is why the use of more than one medium is important. Almost as important as the use of several media to reinforce the information is the reduction of levels through which the information must pass. If at all possible, any spoken information should be given *directly to the person for whom it is meant,* and should not pass through a long chain of command. When it is necessary for information to be passed through several levels, the playback and the use of as many other media as possible is of vital importance. (See drawing.)

SUBJECT: COMPLETION & DELIVERY
OF "S-COAT" TO VICE PRES.
VIA: MISS MARR, MR. LANDAU, MRS JAMES

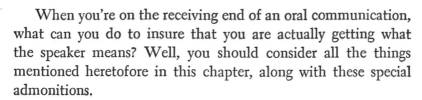

Receiving Information Accurately

When you're on the receiving end of an oral communication, what can you do to insure that you are actually getting what the speaker means? Well, you should consider all the things mentioned heretofore in this chapter, along with these special admonitions.

Listening

Much has already been said about listening in a previous chapter. In receiving information you should listen especially for two things: (a) the speaker's intent, as sometimes opposed to what he actually says—and this often involves his attitude toward what he is saying, and (b) the structure, or number of main points he is making. If you have any doubt as to either of these things, ask for a clarification when the speaker has finished, or when he has reached a transitional point.

Notes and questions

The speaker may be bent upon giving you all the information in one indigestible mass. If he is a person whose thought processes are upset by interruption, then you'll just have to endure his lack of consideration, take notes as rapidly as you can, and then ask questions when he has finished. If, however, he has organized his information well, he shouldn't object to your interrupting to ask that a point be clarified along the way. Try not to ask unnecessary questions; sometimes a receiver is so eager to get every detail that he will clutter communication by asking asinine and unnecessary details. A physician I know impressed upon his new receptionist the necessity for taking down accurately the names of any patients who called. After a few weeks, his patients began to complain about the stupidity of his receptionist, and he learned that the girl was asking *all* patients to spell their names—even such commonplace ones as Smith, Levy,

Brown, Johnson and O'Brien! However, if it seems to you that an important part of an oral communication is not clear, don't hesitate to ask questions to clarify it. It's much better to act the dunce *now*, than to be made a greater dunce later!

Playback

If the person giving you the information does not give you the opportunity to repeat the information he has given you, *ask* for it. This request does not necessarily need to make either of you appear stupid; you simply say, "Excuse me, sir; just so I'll know that I have this information accurately, would you mind if I repeat it?" The chances are you will be doing the giver of information a favor by this action; he may be reminded of something he intended to say and forgot. Don't underestimate the value of the playback; after all, Western Union has *insisted* upon it for decades!

Keep an open mind

All of the admonitions about not jumping to conclusions and about not closing one's mind which have been mentioned in the two previous chapters are applicable to receiving information. It is especially important that you do not pass judgment on the information you are receiving until you have heard *all* of it. You cannot really listen and remember information accurately if you're saying to yourself such things as, "This will never work; it's completely impractical!", "Uh-oh! Personnel is not going to like this!", "He's taking out his spite on the vice president for not inviting him to join the V.P.'s club," or "Boy, he's really boot-licking the boss with this one." Don't pass judgment on what you hear until you have actually heard it *all*. If you receive the information accurately, your later judgment on it will be more accurate. (All of us pass judgment on information we receive, whether or not we admit it.)

Information Versus Commands

A final word to both the giver and the receiver of information in today's business world. There exists today an attitude on the part of both that information should be passed on with this sort of attitude: "Now, get this! Get it quickly. Get it accurately! Get it quickly! Now, remember it! Get it quickly!"

Such an attitude is absurd and unrealistic. Giving information is diametrically opposed to giving military commands. In the military, obeying a command is a reflex action; the receiver of the command has performed the command so often that the words trigger an instant reaction. There is no need to think; one simply acts on an established pattern. In giving and getting *information*, there is a great need, not only to think, but to understand and to exercise patience and tolerance.

A Word
Fitly Spoken

POLONIUS: ... What do you read, my lord?

HAMLET: Words, words, words.

POLONIUS: What is the matter, my lord?

HAMLET: Between who?

POLONIUS: I mean the matter that you read, my lord.

HAMLET: Slanders, sir: for the satirical rogue says here that old men have grey beards, that their faces are wrinkled, their eyes purging thick amber and plum-tree gum, and that they have a plentiful lack of wit, together with most weak hams: all which, sir, though I most powerfully and potently believe, yet I hold it not honesty to have it thus set down, for you yourself, sir, should be old as I am, if like a crab, you could go backward.

POLONIUS (*aside*): Though this be madness, yet there is method in 't. ...

Shakespeare, HAMLET

HAVING trounced words thoroughly as being somewhat unreliable for communication purposes, let us apologize to them in this chapter and talk about the *value* of the right word, spoken at the right time and in the proper context. In English we certainly have enough words to choose from— about 750,000 of them, not including words in specialized dictionaries of science, law, medicine, technical books, slang, and so forth. With so many words at our command we should be able to portray any event graphically, express the finest nuance of emotion, or give the most complicated directions precisely. Alas! Such is not the case, and we have seen some of the reasons why in previous chapters. Here let us talk about *choosing the right* word to say what we mean.

Enlarging Your Vocabulary

Almost everyone believes that he has difficulty in expressing meaning because of a limited vocabulary, and that is partly true. It is manifestly impossible to learn *all* the words in English, as you may have discovered if you have worked many crossword puzzles. Let me say here that knowing the definitions of a lot of words does not guarantee that you will find it easy to express your meaning. Queen Christina of Sweden said of the scholar Salmasius that he knew the word for chair in seven languages, and still did not know how to sit in one! I was once head of a speech department in which a man named Frank taught vocabulary-building. He was literally a walking dictionary, and I never saw him stumped when asked the meaning of any word, however obscure. Everyone marveled at his ability. Then, each instructor was asked to write a syllabus of the courses he taught, and I was appalled at Frank's effort to make the words he knew so well do any useful work for him. He was like Salamasius; his syllabus would not have done justice to an eighth-grade student. So, in building your vocabulary, you should (a) select words that will be useful to you, and (b) know how to use them to your advantage.

Practical suggestions for enlarging your vocabulary

If you wish to acquire a useful vocabulary, resolving to "learn a new word every day" is not going to suffice; you will simply be burdened with a lot of unnecessary words. Besides, I doubt if many of us have the tenacity to stick with such a resolution for 365 days a year. Let me suggest how you can combine pleasure with learning and acquire *several* words a day.

Keep alongside your easy chair a good dictionary, a pad and pencil, and a current magazine that contains factual articles on a variety of subjects. Read one article a day, pencil in hand, and check every word whose meaning you are not absolutely sure of —even though you may be able to guess its meaning from the context. Then, *when you have finished the article,* look up the definitions of the words you have checked. (Don't stop during your reading to do this.) If, upon examining the definitions of the word in your dictionary, you think that the word will not be useful to you in your reading, writing and speaking, forget it. If you believe that the word may be useful to you in expressing your thoughts about your profession, your emotions, actions and opinions, write it down. Now, go back to the article you have read and notice how the word is used. Do *not* write down the definition of the word—just the word itself. Then, tomorrow, before you start to read another article, review the words you jotted down today. If you have forgotten their meanings, look them up again. But let me warn you, do *not* write down their definitions; the emphasis should be on your memorizing the word and its meanings—not on copying a word from the dictionary onto a piece of paper. Review your list of words each day; each recall of the meanings of those words will strengthen your grasp of them.

For this approach to vocabulary-building, I suggested that you use a magazine that has many short articles on a wide variety of subjects. *The Reader's Digest* is ideal, for several reasons: The articles in it are usually short, requiring ten minutes or less to read; the articles encompass a large variety of subjects, including many on human relations; and the vocabulary used in the writing is a simple, workaday one. To present yourself with a bit more of a challenge, you may want to alternate an article from *The Reader's Digest* with an article from a trade magazine of your own profession; later, you may choose some of the magazines with a more esoteric vocabulary. *Time* magazine is always looking for an unusual word with which to express an exact shade of meaning, and *The New Yorker* not only carries articles of fine literary quality but is also a happy hunting ground for the word-hunter.

We have *three vocabularies:* One for reading, one for writing and one for speaking. Our reading vocabulary is the largest, because we can guess at the meaning of an isolated word by the way it is used. Our writing vocabulary is smaller, but is larger than our speaking vocabulary because we can *stop* to *think* of the right word we want to use. Our speaking vocabulary is the smallest, because if the words to express the exact shade of meaning aren't there waiting for us, we fall back on *clichés,* or words which don't quite express what we want to say but which will "make do." How does one increase his speaking vocabulary? My suggestion is that you do it by *writing* and *listening,* which may sound paradoxical.

Try to listen to speeches and discussions by intelligent, educated people on radio and television (Oh, yes—there *are* some!). Note the way they express themselves, and the specific words they use. (Later in this chapter, I will suggest some things to listen *for.*) Even more important than listening to others is to *write* something every day. It doesn't have to be more than a short paragraph, and it can be on any subject: Tell something that happened at the office, write out directions for doing a certain job, express your opinion of a current event, try to express some emotion that was aroused in you during the day. The important thing is that it be something that happened to *you*. When you've written it, go over it and examine it for some of the things we will discuss later; ask yourself if you've used the exact words to express your meaning, or if you could have found a better word. When you've finished the paragraph, put it aside, and don't look at it for a week. Then, reread it and see if you cannot *then* find a way of expressing yourself that would make the paragraph (a) easier to understand, (b) more vivid, (c) more precise in its meaning, and (d) more rhythmic in sound. We improve our vocabulary by *using* words, and you can use them without fear on paper, where you have an opportunity to correct and improve them at a later date. After you have learned to express yourself in writing—after the words have become *yours* —you will find it easier to express yourself in *speaking*. The differential between the speeds of thought and speech explained on Pages 51 and 123 will help you to do this.

Style and Usage

Developing an effective style in speaking is something which I believe must be "caught" rather than taught. It involves cultivating your ear for arrangement of words in a sentence, for arranging sentences in varying lengths to give cadence and rhythm, and finding fresh and vivid imagery to convey your impressions to others. However, there are a few requisites for clear, forthright, communicative speech style which can be taught.

General versus specific

Just as we try to avoid hasty generalizations in understanding people, an effective speaker should avoid general terms if there are specific ones available. Consider the three statements below:

1. *"Mike went across the room."* Now, that doesn't tell us much about the action, does it? Look at the words we might have used to describe Mike's getting from one point to another:

He might have ambled, strutted, shuffled, stumbled, marched, strolled, waddled, plodded, stalked, trudged, tiptoed, sauntered, meandered, strode, glided, trotted, limped or pranced across the room—to name just a few of the ways that would express Mike's movement specifically.

2. *"All liars should have their thumbs cut off with a knife."* If I pretend to have a headache to avoid a dreary party, should my thumbs be amputated? If I evade telling one acquaintance what another acquaintance has said about him in order to avoid hurting him, should I be punished similarly? If I am guilty of misrepresenting the facts slightly when a lady customer asks me how a certain hat suits her, when I know *she* likes it, is this, too, punishable by depriving me of my thumbs? Even witnesses who perjure themselves under oath in court are seldom punished so severely. And why "cut off with a knife"? Wouldn't a hatchet, or a meat-cleaver, or an axe or a razor do just as well?

3. *"Thou shalt not kill."* Does that mean that I must not kill the anopheles mosquito that is bent on giving me malaria? That I must not kill the weeds that are destroying my crop? That I must not kill cows or vegetables to get food? Or does it simply mean that I must not commit murder? Whenever you have a choice between a general term and a specific one, use the *specific* one.

Simple versus complex

There are some exact shades of meaning which can be expressed only by words of several syllables; if this is the case, by all means use long words. There are some thoughts which require an occasional long sentence; if such is needed, do not hesitate to use a lengthy sentence. Most communication, however, oral or written, suffers when big words and endless sentences are used. This is more true of spoken communication than of written communication. When you read something, you may stop to reread it and to ponder on its meaning; when you hear it, you must get the meaning at once or you don't get it at all.

Read the following paragraph aloud and ask yourself what it means. Artemus Ward is asking a young newspaperman by the name of Mark Twain to tell him something about silver mining in Nevada:

> What I was after was this: This vein, or lode, or ledge, or whatever you call it, runs along between two layers of granite, just the same as if it were a sandwich. Very well. Now suppose you go down on that—say a thousand feet, or maybe 1200, it don't really matter—before you drift; and then you start your drifts, some of them across the ledge and others along the length of it, where the sulphurets—I believe they call them sulphurets; though why they should, considering that so far as I can see the main dependence of a miner does not lie, as some suppose, but in which it cannot be successfully maintained, in which the same should not continue, while part and parcel of the same ore—not committed to either in the sense referred to—whereas under different circumstances the most inexperienced among us could not detect it, if it were; or might overlook it, if it did; or scorn the whole idea of such a thing, even though it were demonstrated as such. Am I right?

Now the foregoing is obviously what we term "gobbledygook"; it has no coherence, and was not meant to be understood but to confuse. Following, however, is a sentence (only *one* sentence, mind you) from an actual letter sent out by the United States Department of the Interior; it is in answer to the question, "What is the official definition of the term 'preferential customer'?"

> Unfortunately, when discussing such a subject in general and hypothetical terms, either question or response is apt to give a misleading impression because one or another theoretical or hypothetical factor may be singled out for emphasis and the subject is then prone to be viewed against a set of limited conditions and qualifications which may have little relationship to actual facts and circumstances as they develop and in the light of which the

particular status in fact of a given customer will ultimately have to be determined.

The meaning becomes clear in the foregoing selection *if* one takes time to figure it out; and one is apt to "figure it out" by forming many short sentences mentally. Contrast the two selections below; each says, in effect, the same thing:

1. In promulgating by verbalization your cogitations and psychological observations, beware of platitudinous and ponderous pomposity. Sedulously avoid all polysyllabic decantations and pestiferous profanity. Let your oral profundities have intelligibility and veracious vivacity without rodomontade and thrasonical bombast.

2. In speaking your thoughts and observations on human nature, beware of pompous expressions that others have used. Avoid big words and profanity. Speak clearly, lively and truthfully without affectation.

In choosing your words and phraseology for communicating orally, try to stay in the middle of the road. Don't revert to slang unless you do it facetiously, or to obtain a certain effect; try to avoid polysyllabic words unless they are necessary. Here is a short list of three ways of saying the same thing; you can see that the middle one is the one which would be understood most easily when spoken:

Pompous	*Plain*	*Slang*
1. Expedite the implementation.	Put into practice right away.	Get it done chop-chop.
2. Partake of a sumptuous repast.	Eat a delicious meal.	Swill cool chow.
3. Edifice of habitation (or domcile).	Residence.	Pad.
4. I comprehend your elucidation.	I understand your explanation.	I dig you, Daddy-O!
5. Dreadnaught.	Battleship.	Gun scow.

Denotations and connotations

Words both denote and connote. A word's denotation is its literal meaning; its connotations are the additional meanings it has acquired over the years by being used in certain ways. So, looking up the definition of words will not always tell you how they should be used, unless you have a very fine dictionary and study carefully the dictionary's examples of the words' usage. A good book on usage itself is also helpful.

In teaching a high school class in vocabulary-building (and I consider most courses in vocabulary-building worthless), I asked the students to look up the meanings of five strange words they heard or read each week and use each word in a written sentence. One youngster's sentence puzzled me. It read, "The drunk man walked down the road askance." Upon questioning the student, I learned that the definition for "askance" in his dictionary was "sideways," which might be an understandable way for a drunk to walk down a road. The word literally means "sideways," but it *connotes* turning the head sideways as one often does in questioning or in expressing doubt.

A word or a phrase may connote different things in different situations. Take, for instance, the case of the barber who had just been converted to Christianity and had resolved to try to convert one person every day. His first customer of the day stepped into the barber chair and asked for a shave. The barber put the apron around the customer's face, and then—as he was sharpening his razor—intoned solemnly, "My dear friend, have you asked the Lord to forgive you of your sins?"

Note the somewhat naughty connotation of a perfectly innocent word in this next anecdote.

> Tony, in the fifth grade, asked his teacher what the word "frugal" meant.
>
> "Frugal means to save, Tony," she replied. "Now, see if you

can use the word in a sentence or paragraph. You know, words are useless unless we can make them come to life."

Tony wrote busily for a few minutes, and announced that he had been able to use the word in a short story. The teacher asked him to read to the class what he had written. This is what he read:

"One day a handsome young prince was riding by the side of a swift river. From the middle of the stream he heard a beautiful maiden screaming, 'Frugal me! Frugal me! Frugal me!' And he *did!* And they lived happily ever after."

No restaurant owner would list on his menu an item such as "the rear end of a dead sheep" because of its connotation; he can sell far more orders of that dead sheep by listing it as a "loin lamb chop." Hilda Schmidt operates an excellent restaurant across the road from a du Pont plant along the St. Lawrence River, and—in my opinion—prepares the best *sauerbraten* in Canada. She lists it on the menu as "German pot roast" and it sells out before any other item on the menu. The men from the du Pont plant have tried it, found it delicious, and passed on the word. "But *sauerbraten,*" Hilda told me, "they would not even *try!*"

In the two columns at the end of this paragraph, the expressions opposite each other have the same basic *denotation,* but their *connotations* differ. To illustrate how you, yourself, react to word connotations, select the expression you would prefer being applied to you:

1. He's somewhat erratic.	1. He's unmethodical.
2. It was an infelicitous act.	2. It was a foolish thing to do.
3. He's off-center.	3. He's eccentric.
4. He uses sleight of hand.	4. He exercises skill.
5. She's a gay divorcée.	5. She's a young widow.

Synonyms and antonyms

Have you ever listened to a speaker who used the same word or expression over and over again, until he sounded like a phonograph needle that was stuck in one spot? Well, if you are to avoid being such a person, you had better get yourself a supply of synonyms. For each new word that you learn, it is a good idea to look up its synonyms and its antonyms.[1] Then, in the paragraph you write to improve your vocabulary, see how many synonyms you can work in to avoid repeating the same word. Do the same thing in making a speech or in carrying on a conversation; try to think of words that are definite, whose connotations express the shade of meaning you desire, and try to avoid repeating the same word over and over. Notice in the two paragraphs that follow how other words are substituted for the word "reduced" to relieve the monotony of its repetition. Notice also how much richer in meaning the paragraph becomes when other words are substituted for "reduced."

> I remember the financial depression of the early nineteen-thirties when great wealth was *reduced* to pennies. Our wealthy neighbor, with an estate that cost nearly half a million dollars, was *reduced* to selling it at auction. Circumstances had so *reduced* the cash available to anyone that the estate found a buyer only after its price had been *reduced* to a fraction of its worth. In my own family, my father's income was *reduced* to less than it cost us to live; no matter how hard we tried, we could not *reduce* living expenses below a bare minimum, which was not enough of a *reduction* to keep us out of debt. My proud mother, once the social leader of the community, was *reduced* to the status of a day-laborer.

> I remember the financial depression of the early nineteen thirties when great wealth *dwindled* to pennies. Our wealthy

[1] Just to jog your memory: A synonym is a word with the *same* meaning as another; an antonym is a word with the *opposite* meaning.

neighbor with an estate that cost nearly half a million dollars, was *compelled* to sell it at auction. Circumstances had so *decreased* the amount of cash available to anyone that the estate found a buyer only after its price had been *lowered* to a fraction of its worth. In my own family, my father's income *dropped* to less than it cost us to live; no matter how hard we tried, we could not *cut* living expenses below a bare minimum, which was not enough of a *curtailment* to keep us out of debt. My proud mother, once the social leader of the community, was *debased* to the status of a day-laborer.

Because we are lazy and are imitators of our associates, most of us fall into using the same words we hear others use, without striving to be original. Thus, many people find that they have only about four adjectives: *great, lousy, marvelous* and *terrible.* We use them over and over, while the thesaurus lists dozens and dozens of words which we might substitute to express meaning more exactly and enrich our speech at the same time. Just to give you an example, I selected a few words at random and counted the synonyms for them in *Roget's International Thesaurus.* The results are startling:

Word	Number of Synonyms
Love	404
Hate	107
Drunk	137
Sober	18
Speak	50
Death	360

So you see there is no paucity of words with which to express ourselves; there is only the problem of finding the right one.

Vividness

When you hear someone's speech described as "colorful," what does it bring to mind? Enthusiasm? What the person has to say? Perhaps, but I have heard the most commonplace things spoken of, in a dry-as-dust manner, by people whose speech was as colorful as a maple tree in autumn. One of those people was my old half-Indian, half-Negro "Mammy," who lived with my family for more than fifteen years; here is the way she expressed a couple of things:

> *Noise:* "Louder than a jackass in a tin barn," and "Makes more fuss than a locomotive in a gravel bed."
> *Anger:* "Raring like a ram tied to a gatepost."

While they are homely, they are vivid.
Here are some others:

> 1. An aviator describes himself as flying "where murmurs of the windy world reach upward to the sky."
> 2. A politician describes his opponent as having "a heart as black as a slice out of midnight."
> 3. A reporter describes the collapse of a building as sounding like "thunder tumbling down the stairway of the sky."

Such vivid figures of speech make one's speech colorful.

After having listened critically to literally thousands of speeches—student as well as professional—I am convinced that the most important single element in a good speech style is "action" words and phrases. (The use of the same "action" words and phrases is also a distinction of the good conversationalist.) Listen to the dramatic, enlightening and compelling records *I Can Hear It Now* [2] and you will be impressed by the fact that *almost every sentence* of the brilliant narration, as well as the excerpts from the better speeches, contains some action. Here are a few other examples:

> Democracy is not dying.
> We know it because we have seen it revive—and grow . . .

[2] By Fred Friendly and Edward R. Murrow. Narrated by Mr. Murrow. Columbia Records.

We know it because democracy alone, of all the forms of government, enlists the full force of men's enlightened will.

We know it because democracy alone has constructed an unlimited civilization capable of infinite progress in the improvement of human life.

We know it because, if we look below the surface, we sense it still spreading on every continent—for it is the most humane, the most advanced, and in the very end the most unconquerable of all forms of human society.

—FRANKLIN D. ROOSEVELT (*from his Third Inaugural Address, January 20, 1941*)

Hitler knows that he will have to break us in this Island or lose the war itself. If we can stand up to him all Europe may be free and the life of the world may move forward into broad, sunlit uplands. But if we fail, then the whole world, including the United States, including all that we have known and cared for, will sink into the abyss of a new Dark Ages made more sinister, and perhaps more protracted, by the lights of perverted science. Let us, therefore, brace ourselves to our duties, and so bear ourselves that if the British Empire and its Commonwealth last for a thousand years, men will still say, "This was their finest hour."

—SIR WINSTON CHURCHILL (*Address to the British Parliament, June, 1940*)

A sense of duty pursues us ever. It is omnipresent, like the Deity. If we take to ourselves the wings of the morning, and dwell in the uttermost parts of the sea, duty performed or duty violated, is still with us—for our happiness or our misery. If we say the darkness shall cover us, in the darkness as in the light our obligations are yet with us. We cannot escape their power nor fly from their presence. They are with us in this life; will be with us at its close.

—DANIEL WEBSTER (*Address to the Jury, Knapp-White Murder Case, August 8-20, 1830*)

Word fodder

For you city-dwellers, maybe I should define "fodder." It is food for farm animals, which fills them but gives them little or no nourishment. It is necessary for their comfort, but of little value to their growth or health. In speaking, we have "word-fodder," words which seem necessary only to the inexpert speaker and are totally useless to his hearers. Pray you, avoid them!

Perhaps the most insidious class of "word fodder" is the compound preposition; next in offensiveness is the compound conjunction. Margaret Nicholson writes, "taken as a whole they are almost the worst element in modern English, stuffing up the newspaper columns with a compost of nouny abstractions." [3] Here are a few of these offenders, placed opposite the single word which they replace:

Why *this?* . . . . .when *this* is all that's needed?

in the nature of	like
from the point of view of	for
with the result that	so that
with reference to	about
in the event that	if
with a view to	to
in the process of	of

Other words and phrases which you can do without:

Very. Probably the most overworked and least expressive word in English. How much is "very" much? It says nothing.

Myself. Nineteen times out of twenty, the speaker uses this word ungrammatically. Stay on the safe side and forget about it.

More-or-less. This is worse than "very." As the Scriptures say, let your yea be yea and your nay nay, and don't "more-or-less" your listeners to the point of distraction.

[3] A *Dictionary of American-English Usage*, New American Library, p. 99.

I think. This weakens every sentence in which it is used. In a democratic society you have a right to think, and to speak your thoughts. Speak them without weakness. Contrast for strength the two sentences which follow:

> I think that we should pave this street.
> We should pave this street.

Foreign words and phrases

We have brought into our English vocabulary many words and phrases from other languages. We stubbornly Anglicize the pronunciation of some of them, and make an awkward attempt to preserve the original pronunciation of others. Because of the differences between English and other languages (shape of lips, tongue positions, rhythms and intonations), it is almost impossible to pronounce correctly a foreign word dropped casually into the middle of an otherwise all-English sentence. So, if you have a choice between using an English expression and a foreign one, use English *if* it expresses precisely what you mean. Sometimes a foreign word is used for the sake of brevity: Instead of saying, "Each item on the menu must be paid for separately," it's much simpler to say, "It's an *à la carte* menu." At the end of this chapter I have listed fifty of these foreign words and phrases which you are likely to hear or read, with their meanings and an attempt to approximate their pronunciation phonically.

Technical words

Do not be awed by technical words if they are words from an occupation other than your own. Try not to use technical words from your own occupation when talking with a layman, unless you must use them for brevity's sake; when you use them, explain their meaning to the layman.

Reference Books

Choosing a dictionary

Every business and professional man should have access to a good dictionary. The many on the market vary in scope and usefulness. A good, unabridged dictionary is ideal, but if you settle for one of the smaller volumes, examine it carefully for these features:

1. *Word coverage.* How many entries does it have? Does it contain new words that have been added to our language in recent years? Does it contain synonyms and antonyms to words? Does it give the derivation and changes in meaning a word has undergone (etymology)? Does it give the usage of the word, i.e., does it give phrases which use the word? Does it contain a section on American idioms? When was it last revised?

2. *Pronunciation.* Does it make clear which pronunciation of a word (when there are more than one) is preferable? Does it distinguish between American and British pronunciations? Is its key to pronunciation easily understood and convenient to find?

3. *Definitions.* Does it indicate the most universal meaning of words, and then give their more obscure and specialized meanings? Does it "pass the buck" on word definitions by referring you to other words?

4. *Extra features.* Is the type large and readable, and the paper opaque enough to hide the print on the reverse side of the sheets? Does it contain extra features such as a pronouncing gazetteer, a section on slang, biographical section, and section on foreign expressions?

You are not likely to find *all* these features in any one of the smaller dictionaries, but look for those which will be most useful for you. Below I have listed five of the most popular abridged dictionaries; the first two have the largest coverage of words, while the last two rank higher in readability.

1. *Webster's New Collegiate Dictionary.* G. & C. Merriam Co.

2. *New College Standard Dictionary.* Funk & Wagnalls.

3. *The Winston Dictionary, College Edition.* John C. Winston Co.

4. *The American College Dictionary.* Random House.

5. *Macmillan's Modern Dictionary.* The Macmillan Co.

Specialized books on words

The Macmillan dictionary is a bit sketchy on etymology, so you may want to supplement it with an etymological dictionary. I recommend Walter W. Skeat's *A Concise Etymological Dictionary of the English Language,* published by Oxford University Press.

If you are in doubt about proper usage of words and parts of speech, an invaluable book is *A Dictionary of American-English Usage Based on Fowler's Modern English Usage* by Margaret Nicholson. It is now available in a paperback edition published by Signet Books.

If you wish a handy book which gives at a glance the preferred pronunciation of a number of English words, *The NBC Handbook of Pronunciation* compiled by James Bender, is excellent. Perhaps the most useful book on pronunciation is the Kenyon & Knott *Pronouncing Dictionary of American English,* but you need to know the International Phonetic Alphabet in order to use it. An occasional dip into these books will be well worth your effort, for you will learn something each time you turn a page, and will eventually recognize the truth of the passage of Scripture:

"A word fitly spoken is like apples of gold in pictures of silver." (*Proverbs* 25:11)

Words Frequently Mispronounced

Here is a list of words which are often mispronounced. Most of them are common words which we read or hear every day, although I have included a few whose pronunciation is at such variance with their spelling that they need special attention. It's a safe bet that most college graduates will mispronounce at least one-third of these words, if you take as your authority one of the pronouncing dictionaries which lists preferred pronunciations.

Abdomen	Champion	Dictionary
Absorb	Chaos	Diphtheria
Absurd	Chasm	Discretion
Acclimate	Chastisement	Docile
Address (*n.*)	Chocolate	Drama
Address (*v.*)	Comely	Drowned
Adult	Comptroller	Eccentric
Alias	Conversant	Err
Ally	Combatant	Epitome
Almond	Comfortable	Exigency
Amateur	Comparable	Extraordinary
Architect	Condolence	Exquisite
Aristocratic	Consummate (*adj.*)	Film
Arctic	Corps	Finale
Athlete	Cuisine	Finance
Auspices	Dais	Financier
Aviation	Data	Forehead
Bade	Decadence	Formidable
Bottle	Decorative	Frequented
Bravado	Decorous	Gala
Breeches	Defects	Gallant
Brooch	Deluge	Gamut
Cache	Demise	Garage
Caramel	Despicable	Gentlemen
Cerebral	Desultory	Genuine
Chagrin	Diamond	Gesture

Gratis	Luxury	Ribald
Grievous	Memorable	Rinse
Harass	Mischievous	Robust
Height	Municipal	Romance
Heinous	Museum	Rouge
Horizon	Obligatory	Sacrilegious
Hospitable	Often	Schism
Hostile	Orchestra	Scourge
Human	Orgy	Secretary
Humble	Particularly	Senile
Ignominy	Peculiarly	Short-lived
Impious	Penalize	Similarly
Impotent	Perilous	Solace
Inclement	Pique	Status
Incognito	Poem	Strength
Incomparable	Positively	Subtle
Influence	Precedence	Superfluous
Inquiry	Precedent	Tarpaulin
Irrelevant	Presentation	Theatre
Irremediable	Primarily	Tribunal
Irreparable	Quay	Tribune
Irrevocable	Quasi	Tuesday
Italian	Quintuplets	Unrequited
Jugular	Radiator	Unguent
Juvenile	Recognize	Vagary
Lamentable	Reconnaissance	Vehement
Length	Remonstrate	Virile
Library	Reptile	Whore
Literature	Research	Yeast
Longevity	Respite	Zealot

Foreign Words and Phrases

In this section there are fifty-odd foreign words and phrases which you will hear often in English. Some of them are so common that I have not bothered to give definitions for them. In order to approximate their pronunciations, I have resorted to "phonic" spelling rather than using diacritical markings. Accented syllables are in capital letters. This necessitates two observations: (a) when a letter of the alphabet is used as a separate syllable, it is to be pronounced as it is sounded when repeating the English alphabet; (b) a tilde [añ] above a syllable indicates that the syllable should be nasalized. I advise that you listen to someone who knows the language from which the words come before using them in public. (The Latin words are an exception; no one really *knows* how Latin was pronounced!)

Word	*Pronunciation*	*Definition*
Ad infinitum	ADD-in-fin-I-tuhm	To infinity; too many times to be counted.
Aficionado	ah-feeth-ee-o-NAH-doh	An enthusiast about something; specifically, a bull fight follower.
Alma Mater	AL-muh MAY-tuh or AHL-muh MAH-tuh	"Our Mother." Today, it means the school or college from which one graduates.
Aria	AHR-ih-uh	A solo, or melody, sung in the course of an opera.
Attaché	at-tash-A	A member of a diplomatic staff.
Blasé	blah-ZAY	Jaded; one who has seen everything and done everything; cynical.

Word	*Pronunciation*	*Definition*
Bona fide	BO-nah FI-dih	Genuine; "in good faith."
Bourgeois	boorzh-WAH	The lower middle class.
Bouquet	boo-KAY	
Carte blanche	KAHRT BLAHNSH	"White paper"; write your own ticket; complete freedom.
Cello	CHELL-O	A musical instrument, similar to the violin but larger.
Chauffeur	sho-FURR	
Chef	SHEFF	
Chic	SHEEK	Smart in appearance; stylish.
Cliché	klee-SHAY	An expression that is trite; that has been used until it is tired.
Clique	KLEEK	A group of people banded together for a common purpose.
Concerto	kuhn-CHAIR-toh	A solo, accompanied by the full orchestra.
Corps	KOHR	
Coupon	KOO-pahn	(We have half-Anglicized this.)
Cuisine	kwih-ZEEN	Cooking—refers to the type of food and the way it is prepared.
Debris	day-BREE	Rubbish; clutter; scattered remnants of destruction.
Debut	DAY-byoo	One's first appearance in a new role.

Word	*Pronunciation*	*Definition*
Deluxe	dih-LUKS	Luxurious; the finest.
Dossier	DOH-SEE-A	A file on one person or project, containing all important information.
Elite	a-LEET	"The cream of the crop"; the select few, in any group.
En masse	ãh-MAHS	All together; in a group, as a whole.
Ennui	AHN-WEE	Boredom over an extended period.
En route	AHN ROOT	
Ensemble	ãh-SAHMBL	An outfit that harmonizes perfectly: clothes, music, or members of a staff.
Faux pas	FO-PAH	An embarrassing error.
Fiancé (*male*)	fee-AHN-SAY	The person to whom one is engaged to be married.
Fiancée (*female*)		
Forte	FORT *or* FOUR-tay	One's strong point. In music, loud, powerful.
Gala	GAY-luh	Gay, festive.
Laissez faire	LEZZ-A FAIR	"To let alone." Not to interfere, especially in politics.
Liaison	lee-yeh-ZOH	A connection, usually in love or politics; private understanding.
Lingerie	LAE-zhur-ee	Feminine underwear of delicate construction.

Word	Pronunciation	Definition
Memoir	MEHM-wahr	An autobiography; one's written recollection of past events.
Naive	nah-EEVE	Childlike; unsophisticated.
Per se	PURR SEE	Standing alone; taken out of context. As, "The act *per se* was not evil, but it led to evil consequences."
Penchant	PENN-chuhnt	An especial fondness for something; an indulgence.
Post mortem	POST MOR-tim	Literally, something done after someone else has died; it connotes any examination of an event after it has occurred.
Prima donna	PREEM-uh DAH-nuh	"First lady." The star female singer in opera; a temperamental person who must always be first.
Prima facie	PRY-muh FAY-shih	First appearance; evidence enough to establish a case in law unless refuted.
Protégé	PRO-tuh-zhay	A person whom one protects, teaches and promotes in his career.
Rendezvous	RAHN-day-voo	A meeting by appointment; often a regular meeting by lovers.
Repertoire	REHP-uh-twahr	The numbers an artist (singer or actor or musician) can perform.

Word	Pronunciation	Definition
Schmaltz	SHMAWLTS	Extremely sentimental expression in music or art.
Surveillance	sir-VAY-luhns	A close inspection.
Tête-à-tête	TATE-ah-TATE	"Head to head." A private party for two.
Via	Vy-uh or VEE-uh	By way of a certain route or certain means.
Vice versa	VY-sih VERS-uh	"The opposite is also true."
Vis-à-vis	VEEZ-ah-VEE	Face to face.

Here are a few examples of the usage of foreign phrases or words. Don't use them as often as I have in these sentences, or people will think you are "word dropping"!

1. Carlyle said, "Man is the noblest creation of God, and *vice versa.*"

2. The *prima donna* sang a beautiful *aria,* and was then accompanied by a male *ensemble.*

3. The *blasé* person is one who pretends that life is full of *ennui.*

4. The naval *attaché* was *naive* enough to swear that the embassy he served harbored spies or other persons engaged in *surveillance.*

5. Mendelssohn's *Violin Concerto* is happy music for a *gala* occasion.

6. Catherine the Great was supposed to have a *penchant* for handsome, young soldiers, and frequently invited one for a *tête-à-tête.*

7. Malvina Hoffman was a *protégée* of the great sculptor, Rodin.

8. The Monroe Doctrine advocated a policy of *laissez faire* for all nations.

9. Will your new *chef* demand *carte blanche* in planning the *cuisine* of your restaurant?

10. In his *memoirs* (1828), Casanova wrote openly of political and amatory *liaisons* which he enjoyed. He scorned the *bourgeois*, but kept *rendezvous* with many of the *élite* personages of the time, including Madame Pompadour. Restraint was not Casanova's *forte*, and his *memoirs* are the *dossier* of a professional lover, possessing a masterly *repertoire* of love's tricks. It is said that he once made a *faux pas*, however: V*is-à-vis* with a half-undressed noblewoman, he commented on her poor taste in *lingerie*.

11. Her *fiancé* presented her a *bona fide* gift certificate for a *deluxe* set of crystal.

12. The town turned out *en masse* for the *debut* of the young *cellist*; only a small *clique* of jealous musicians stayed away.

13. A *cliché* is a colorful expression that has lost its lustre from being repeated *ad infinitum*.

14. The detachment of cavalry *corps* specialists had to travel *via* Tivoli because the direct route was blocked by *debris*.

Chapter Five

Developing
Self-Confidence

Fear defeats more men than any other one thing in the world. —ELBERT HUBBARD

NAPOLEON said that of the four elements constituting an army—size, training, equipment and morale—*morale* was worth more than the other three put together. Your personal morale—your self-confidence—is worth as much as any of your other skills in communicating with others successfully. This chapter will explore two areas of personal morale: (a) the transitory lack of self-confidence which we shall call stage fright, which afflicts most of us at some time, and (b) the deeper and more serious sense of inadequacy which abides with some people constantly, a feeling of inferiority.

96

Stage Fright

You go into the boss's office to ask for a raise in salary, or you are called upon to make a speech before your Kiwanis Club; the blood rushes to your head and you forget what you were going to say, your mouth gets dry, your knees start to shake and your voice trembles as you stutter and stammer to release a few words. In short, you're a wreck. You have stage fright. What is it and how can it be controlled? Before I try to answer those questions, let me say three things concerning stage fright: first, if you have it, you are never going to get rid of it completely; second, a certain amount of it is desirable in a vital speaker; third, it *can* be controlled.

What is it?

Stage fright is fear, no different from any other fear. Just above your kidneys are a pair of glands called the adrenal glands; they manufacture one of the most powerful organic stimulants known to man, adrenalin. When adrenalin is introduced into the liver, it causes that organ to manufacture blood sugar at a rapid rate. This gives you excess energy which you cannot use physically if you are sitting at a conference table or standing before an audience. How many times have you seen a speaker *try* to work off that energy by twisting his fingers, pacing back and forth on the platform, clearing his throat or putting his hands in his pockets and withdrawing them constantly?

As uncomfortable as they may make you, don't judge those adrenal glands too harshly. Nature put them in your body for the purpose of giving you extra energy and strength when you need it—to batter down a locked door and escape from a burning building, for instance. It is not idle supposition that people possess added strength when they are frightened or angry; in crises, men have often performed superhuman feats of strength and stamina. After these feats have been accomplished, the performer is usually completely exhausted, for he has burned up a tremendous amount of physical and nervous energy. Nature has, however, given him an emergency supply of strength to help him survive. Recently I read in a newspaper that a housewife weighing less than a hundred pounds had not only pulled a drowning man out of the ocean, but had dragged him fifty yards away from the water's edge and administered artificial respiration until he revived; the man weighed nearly three hundred pounds!

Why must you keep it?

Why is stage fright difficult to overcome? Well, let's take a look at the anxiety we have when we first operate a strange mechanical apparatus. Suppose that you have just bought a new color television set, and you invite your neighbors in to look at a special program. The set requires some adjustments in order to perform well, and you experience some concern and anxiety as you make them. Your pride and ego are at stake; you want desperately for the machine to justify your judgment in purchasing it, and so you have a slight case of stage fright. Later, when you have learned the eccentricities of the machine—when you know exactly which knob to turn to clear up each channel— you operate the machine for outsiders to see without the least bit of discomfort. When I was learning to fly, I was scared almost to the point of regurgitation on my first solo flight. Later, beyond checking routine things, I took off on hundreds of solo flights with no more concern than it takes to put a piece of bread into a toaster.

We lose our stage fright when we are working with mechanical things, because they remain essentially the same day after day. People, on the other hand, change almost momentarily. They are always and forever strangers. Your boss is not the same as he was yesterday, and he will not be the same tomorrow; he is changed by what happens to him on any particular day. Though you have been married to the same wife for fifteen years, and believe that you know precisely how she will react to any situation, you still get an occasional surprise. There is always an element of the unknown in other people, and we fear the unknown. That is why, although you may overcome the fear in operating a strange mechanical device, you may never fully overcome your fear of the unknown when talking with people.

If you have stage fright, you travel with very distinguished company. Madame Ernestine Schumann-Heink, who had one of the greatest successful singing careers of any artist in this century (and certainly the longest—more than fifty years), declared that she had stage fright each time she stepped onto a stage and that it never abated during her entire career. I have known intimately dozens of professional performers in the entertainment world, and most of them tell me that they are petrified with fear before each performance. After twenty-five years of teaching in college, I confess that before meeting a new class for the first time, I perspire so profusely that my shirt is soaked from my armpits down to my belt!

THE BOSS

LAST WEEK—
AN ANGEL

YESTERDAY—
A DEVIL

TO-DAY—
A FRIEND

TO-MORROW—
WHAT?

Why you should like it

No one except a masochist enjoys being uncomfortable, and fright certainly makes us uncomfortable, but it has its advantages and uses. If you are completely indifferent to other people's esteem—if you just don't give a hang about their interests and opinions—you probably will have no stage fright in talking with them. They, in turn, will sense your indifference, and this will affect their reception of your ideas. The process of communicating is a give-and-take situation; in talking with others, one receives just about as much as he gives. If you give your listener complete indifference, that is what you will receive.

What about the *usefulness* of this nervous energy in talking with people? Empathy is the physical response one person returns when stimulated by another. If controlled, the bodily tonus generated by a minor degree of stage fright can help hold a listener's attention and can give your listener the physical feeling that you are "stimulating." So, don't worry too much about *having* stage fright. Instead, concentrate on how to *control* it.

Physical control

When your adrenal glands start overworking because of fear, they cause you to fidget and squirm, which scares you even more, which causes the adrenal glands to work harder, which causes more physical discomfort in you, which causes the glands to ... It's a vicious cycle, and you must break it somewhere, so you may as well attempt some physical measures which have helped other people to control their stage fright. The following suggestions are not "sure cures," but they will help.

1. Keep your breathing deep and slow. About a minute before you are scheduled to speak, inhale fully and *slowly* on a count of, "One ... two ... three ... four." Hold your breath for a

count of two, then exhale slowly on a count of three. Never let your breathing get rapid and shallow. I have heard a flight surgeon say that he could bring down a patient's blood pressure noticeably (but temporarily, of course) by having the patient lie flat on his back and breathe deeply and slowly for a few minutes. If necessary, pencil this reminder on the outline of your speech, or on the margin of the notes you bring into the conference room: "Pause! Breathe deeply!" It will help.

2. At the beginning of your speech—or shortly before—engage in some *planned*, controlled physical activity. If there is a blackboard on the platform, erase it vigorously; move the lectern forward or backward; grip the edge of the lectern or table firmly three or four times and then let your hands fall loosely to your sides; turn through the pages of a magazine or examine the contents of your purse before walking up to the platform; if you can do nothing else, blow your nose! The important thing is to go through some activity which you have planned, and the more strenuous it is, the better it will help you to gain control of your physical mechanism.

Professional actors use an exercise which they claim helps to relieve tension before they go onstage. They bend forward from their hips, with their head and arms hanging loosely toward the floor; then they move their shoulders up and down, shaking the upper part of their trunk and keeping their head and arms dangling as loosely as if those members belonged to a rag doll. I have seen many a glamorous actress give herself such a violent shaking five seconds before smoothing her coiffure and walking into the spotlights looking as cool as a rainbow trout in a mountain stream.

Mental control

Be prepared. The speaker who depends upon the inspiration of the moment for something to say on an important occasion is inviting disaster, whether the occasion is a public speech or a business conference. If you have prepared carefully what you intend to say, and—this is important—if you have rehearsed it *aloud* at least twice, you are already on second base. When you verbalize an idea, it becomes a part of you; you can always say it again, under almost any circumstance. Particularly important, if a formal speech stage-frightens you, is that you memorize your beginning and ending. Knowing how you are going to end is as important as knowing how to begin—maybe more so. You may have to change your opening because of some unexpected introduction or happening, and you should be prepared for that; if you know your ending—your destination—you can get there somehow.

2. Examine your attitude toward people in general, and audiences in particular. Hundreds of times, students have said to me, "I have no trouble in talking to one or two people, but I'm completely lost if I have to speak to a large audience." Why? A large audience is only one person, multiplied by twenty, fifty, or a hundred. If he is armed with the proper weapon, one man can kill you as easily as twenty can. Another lament I hear is, "I can talk very well if I'm seated, but I can't stand up and deliver a speech." Again, why? If your listeners are inclined to slaughter you, you are in a much better position to escape if you are standing! The hard truth is that a person who claims he cannot talk well before a group of people is equally ineffective in talking with one or two people. He is simply not *aware* of his shortcomings when talking with a small group. Subconsciously, he knows that one or two people will be too polite to confront him with his inadequacy, while a crowd—taking cowardly refuge in their number—might not hesitate to discuss his failure.

Ask yourself how *you* regard your audience: Are they a collection of hypercritical, uncharitable, hostile, vicious scandalmongers, ready to tear you to pieces for the slightest slip of your tongue? Of course they are not! Isn't it rather uncharitable on your part to regard them as such? In 999 cases out of 1,000, the members of an audience *want* a speaker to succeed. In the first place, they want you to succeed because they don't want to be bored; in the second place they don't want to be embarrassed, and *they* will be if *you* are. In your home, you try to make a guest comfortable; do the same for your listeners, for—when you are speaking to a large or small group—*you are the host.*

A civilian personnel director at a large military installation was called upon to make a speech to all the "top brass" on the base, plus a number of visiting "bigwigs." She confided to me, "I'm scared blue! First of all, I'm a woman, presuming to tell men older than I how to handle personnel. Secondly, I'm a civilian—and you know how the military regard civilians."

"You know your job and you talk about it interestingly," I reassured her. "Forget that your audience will be high-ranking officers and think of them as people. Remember that every man steps into his trousers one leg at a time. Look over your audience and try to imagine each one of them stepping into his pants, stuffing in his shirttail and then taking his dentures out of the glass where they have soaked during the night."

"Oh, I couldn't do that!" she gasped. But she told me later that my audacious suggestion came to her mind as she walked onto the platform to deliver her speech and caused her to giggle. Since it was a serious occasion, the giggle compelled her to confess her fright and tell the audience of officers about the advice I had given her. They looked at one another, picturing how each had gotten into his uniform that morning, and roared with laughter. My friend's speech got off to a fine start; the actual content of the speech, and her sincerity, made the high-ranking officers realize that she was an expert even though she was a female civilian. The little exchange of laughter at the beginning broke the ice, and erased the "military" and "civilian" labels from everybody's mind.

Feeling Inferior

The average person is often frightened for the first few minutes of talking with others; if he makes some effort to control this fright and adopts a wholesome attitude toward his listeners, his fear will disappear within minutes. There are people who have such a deep-seated sense of inadequacy (inferiority complex) that they find almost any human relationship painful. Extreme cases need professional psychiatric help. Most of us need only to have the sources of feelings of inferiority pointed out to us, combined with determination to face reality, to achieve self-confidence.

Self-confidence is a determination to use our abilities to their fullest extent, to expand our limitations, and to forget the past without regret in order to face the promise of the future. Wow! That's a pretty big order, isn't it? But not an impossible one for the average human being. In the next few paragraphs let's examine some of the reasons people have permanent feelings of inadequacy and what can be done about them.

Social inferiority

You may have been born on the wrong side of the tracks, or into a racial minority. You may have had to peddle papers after school, while other classmates edited the school paper or became stars on the school's football team. You may not have had the clothes or the sportscar to enable you to date Mamie Schwartz, who lived in the mansion on the hill, although you knew Mamie preferred you to the other boys who *were* able to date her. You may have had to work in the college cafeteria to pay your tuition, while your classmates participated in fraternity dances and achieved social status on campus. These are tough experiences for a youngster to survive *at the time he undergoes them,* for he cannot see their ultimate value. But if these things happened to you, THERE IS NOTHING YOU CAN DO

TODAY TO CHANGE THEM! What you can do is to be careful that such minor hardships do not make you a snob.

Now, a snob is not a person who thinks that he is better than other people; rather, he is a person who has allowed himself to be confined within a certain area because he fears to break those confines, and consequently feels the necessity to "downgrade" ("denigrate" for you vocabulary-builders!) everything outside his confines. Here are some typical statements of people whose band of appreciation will not stretch beyond their narrow conditioning—they are snobs!

> "Hillbilly music, indeed! How anyone can bear to listen to it for an instant is beyond me. I'll admit that folk music was a primitive form of good music which developed from it later, but to stay in the mud with it while there are such sublime compositions as those of Mozart, Beethoven and Sibelius to listen to is indicative of a return to the stone age."

> "What's this classical music 'kick' everybody is on today? It's not normal! Nobody really enjoys that longhaired noise! They just pretend to like it because it's supposed to be high class. Me, I'm honest, and don't make any pretenses; give me some good old Irving Berlin tunes or some lively jazz. They're not phony!"

> "Now he's got educated and he goes to art galleries on Sunday, instead of going out to the baseball game. Imagine that? Art galleries!"

> "Really! To spend one's time in a seething mass of smelly, sweating bodies! To pay one's money to watch dumb brutes knock a ball around and to go wild over who catches it or who doesn't, while some other brute is running around a course like a racehorse, is more than I can endure. Look at the opportunities we have to uplift the human race! Just last Sunday at the Metropolitan Museum of Art I saw...."

Now you can depend upon it, something that has given as *many* people as much pleasure, over as long a period of time as folk music has, *must* have some value. The same can be said of classical music, art and baseball. The danger in a feeling of inferiority arising from social disadvantages is that it may take the form of snobbery. If you guard against that, you have nothing to fear.

A young lawyer came to me for help in improving his diction. I considered his speech excellent and, after giving him a number of diction tests, could find nothing substandard about it. What was his real problem? He had been born to immigrant Jewish parents and reared in a poor section of the lower East Side, and had worked his way through college and law school. All the other members of the law firm in which he was practising were sons of wealthy parents; all were also graduates of Ivy League colleges. My student was *afraid* to use the excellent diction he had acquired over the years; he was sure that his partners, knowing his background, would think him affected.

You cannot change the past, and you can't always control the present, but you can push the past into its proper perspective and you can face the present realistically.

Minor physical defects

One of the most irrational causes of a feeling of inadequacy is an imaginary physical defect, or even a genuine *minor* physical defect. I had a roommate in college who was painfully self-conscious because he had red hair, even though it was a splendid head of hair. Apparently minor physical defects disturb us more than major ones. If you are totally blind, if you lose a limb or become paralyzed, you adjust to these catastrophes because you *must*, but it's the little foxes that destroy the vines. You are overweight, or skinny, or have a bad complexion, or you're just downright homely!—and one of these things gives you a feeling of inferiority. What can you do about it? Well, nowadays the science of cosmetics has advanced to the point where most people can be given a presentable appearance, and you owe it to the people who have to look at you to appear as pleasant as possible.

However, if your minor physical defect cannot be changed, try to look at it in this way: "If I am not worth more than this sorry little defect, then I'm a pretty poor specimen of the human race. If I can't change the way I look, then I will compensate for it by developing those *desirable* traits of character and personality which I have." I am sure that, during his first two terms as President of the United States, Franklin Delano Roosevelt was never thought of as a cripple; he had qualities that were *worth so much more* than his affliction that his physical handicap seemed insignificant.

Feeling of guilt

A psychiatrist told me that he considered a useless feeling of guilt to be one of the greatest hindrances to happiness and accomplishment of the American male. In training children, grownups exaggerate the child's misdemeanor into a felony and cause the child to feel more guilty than he should. Lest the child forget a lesson in behavior which the grownup has taught him, the grownup is constantly dragging up mistakes the child has made in the past, thereby deepening his sense of guilt. Once the child has become accustomed to carrying such a burden, he comes to accept it as being a part of him, and the habit of feeling unduly guilty over each mistake goes with him through life.

Mrs. Barrett was a "God-fearing and good" woman, but ignorant and fearful. When she caught her nine-year-old daughter masturbating, she punished the child severely. On the child's second offense the punishment was increased, coupled with the threat, "God will strike you *dead* if you do that!" The child was not detected again, but each time Mrs. Barrett suspected her, she was threatened with punishment by a vengeful God. When the child was twelve years old, she disappeared from school one day and could not be found. Nearly two days later, members of a search party discovered the child, half dead from hunger and exposure, in a dense canebrake miles from town. She had experienced her first menstrual period and—having been told nothing about how her body should function—was terrified. This was certain evidence that God was about to wreak His vengeance on her for her misdemeanor! She had run away desperately so that she should not be exposed as a degenerate and bring shame on her family. Mrs. Barrett showed great relief that the child had been found, but immediately began to shame her for causing the community so much trouble!

Certainly we should learn from our mistakes, but we should not drag them out periodically and brood over them. As in the case of past social disadvantages, there is nothing you can do to change past mistakes, but there is no stain on the future. To-morrow is a blank page; write on it with self-confidence.

Part Two

Person to Person

Chapter Six

Good Conversation Is No Accident

WHEN you are invited to dinner—or to a small party—do you ask who the other guests will be? If you know who else will be present, do you consider what might be talked about, and what you are going to say? Do you ever plan a few questions which you might ask?"

"Heavens, no!" you exclaim; "that would take all the joy—all the spontaneity—out of conversation."

When you invite people to your home, do you tell each one who else will be there, and a little something about each person?

"Wouldn't that be rude?" you ask, and my answer is: Not if you want to help your guests enjoy each other's conversation.

Good conversation is an art, with techniques as definite as those of public speaking or baking a cake. I never regarded it as such until 1947. I was fortunate in that I had always been curious, had read omnivorously, and had been thrown with a variety of people, ranging from backwoods 'possum hunters through Naval officers and college professors to concert artists. I had little difficulty in exchanging pleasant talk with any of them, and never stopped to wonder how it was done. In 1947, I was hired to teach speech to a large number of ex-G.I.s who were enrolled in commercial courses. These ex-servicemen bombarded me constantly with one question: "How do you carry on a good social conversation?" I could not answer them, because I had never examined the technique of good talk.

I am curious, and that curiosity has been disciplined by both military and academic requirements, so I started doing "fun-research" on the subject of conversation. "Fun-research" is working on a project simply to satisfy one's own curiosity, but using the same methods used in ordinary research—the drudgery one endures for an advanced academic degree: I went to the world's largest reference library and read everything I could find on conversation—which was almost nothing; I enrolled in a correspondence course in "The Art of Conversation" (truthfully, it wasn't bad; some of the material in this chapter is stolen from it!); and I asked questions of a great many people. Thus, I evolved some theories about good social talk and good social talkers.

These theories had to be experimented with and tested, so I browbeat a few friends into visiting my speech classes, and persuaded my employer to hire some professional actors and entertainers to visit them also. In each case, the visitor was asked to talk with a few of the students, while the rest of us observed and took notes. I was dismayed by the ineptness of both the visitor and the adult student in conversing interestingly and intelligently. They always excused themselves by proclaiming, "When you put us up on a platform and tell us to talk, it is an unnatural situation; I do much better in a *real* social situation." I was not convinced.

During the next few months, I accepted greedily all the social invitations I received. Some of the hosts were: one of America's most famous actresses, a renowned British man of letters, the president of a chain of banks, a woman who was once the highest-paid female fiction writer in the world, a prominent aviatrix and socialite, the president of a Dutch export company, an art critic and international editor, and a renowned patroness of music. In each case, I was bold enough to ask these hosts what, if any, advance preparation they made for social talk upon being invited out. Some of their responses were enlightening:

It's frightening to think that one's social and cultural background won't provide him with enough material to hold his own in any kind of talk *without* considering what he is to say in advance. However, I do find it necessary to give some thought to what I am going to talk about, as soon as I know who the other guests are.

I ransack my mind for ideas, as soon as I know who is going to be present; I review what I've read or heard about his or her business or occupation. Doesn't everybody do this?

I certainly don't make out a list of topics I can talk about, as I would make out a shopping list! Often, I *do* reread certain sections of the weekly newsmagazines, to familiarize myself with what is going on in—well, let's say the field of medicine—if I know a doctor is going to be present.

When I invite guests to my home, I make it a point to tell them who is going to be there, so that they can surmise what turn the talk may take. That is only common courtesy.

Later, I conducted an intensive inquiry involving 120 people who were commended by their friends as being good conversationalists; 60 per cent of them said that they always gave forethought to possible topics of conversation in any gathering they were about to attend. I have continued this "fun-research" to the moment of writing this. After I have heard a conversation, I ask myself, "What made it dull?" or "Why was it interesting?"

I have also asked the same questions after viewing the many conversation programs that appear on television nowadays.

Getting Started

Let us assume that you are invited to the home of a friend. When you arrive, your friend introduces you to a stranger and leaves the two of you alone while she goes to make coffee. How do you start to talk? Be honest with yourself, and write down three methods you might try, before reading further.

1. ....
   ....
   ....
2. ....
   ....
   ....
3. ....
   ....
   ....

Before we evaluate your methods of starting conversation with a reticent stranger, here are a couple of samples for you to pass judgment upon:

    YOU: Where are you from?

    HE: Paterson, New Jersey.

    YOU: Now, where, exactly, is Paterson?

    HE: It's on the Garden State Parkway, about twelve miles west of the George Washington Bridge.

YOU: Sounds like an interesting town. How big is it?

HE: Oh, I think the population is almost 200,000.

YOU: Gee! I had no idea it was so large.

HE: Yes, it's a good-sized town.

(*Long silence; you try again.*)

YOU: What sort of work do you do?

HE: I'm in insurance.

YOU: That's interesting. What sort of insurance? And, do you sell it, or what?

Is this a conversation? No!

Now, consider this one:

YOU: Boy! that snow is really coming down—big, wet flakes.

HE: Yes, it has been a severe winter.

YOU: Not as tough as the winter of 1948; it got murderously cold then.

HE: I don't remember. But—in the long run—I prefer winter to summer, don't you?

YOU: Yes, I suppose so. That summer of 1957 really *got* me. All the electrical power in New York City went dead because so many people were using their air conditioners. Remember?

HE: No, I don't. You see, I don't live here; I'm only visiting.

YOU: Oh? Where do you live?

HE: Paterson, New Jersey.

YOU: Now where, exactly, is Paterson?

And you are again on the Garden State Parkway, but are you *getting* anywhere, conversationally? A conversation is somewhat like an airplane flight; one of the danger points is the take-off. It is important to get started talking early. If you want to know why, read Robert Benchley's hilarious essay on pushing an elevator bell. How do you get off the ground?

Suppose we start with the negative side; here are some ways *not* to start:

"Don'ts"

1. Don't talk about the weather. There is a reason why many people try to use this as a starter: They are trying to find something in common, and weather is something which everyone has in common in a given locality. The objection to it as a conversation piece is that it can lead nowhere. After all, it can only be hot, cold, wet, dry, windy or calm, and when you have commented on prevailing conditions, you've had it! Another reason for avoiding weather as an opener is that it can be subtly offensive to the other person; it implies that he is blind, deaf, and insensitive to heat, cold, humidity and aridity. So, don't start with the weather—unless it is raining daffodils!

2. Do not open a conversation with a stranger by complimenting his or her clothes. This is not only a breach of etiquette, but is poor psychologically; people wear clothes to make *themselves* attractive, not to show off the clothes. You can make a stranger extremely unhappy if you refer to his raiment and he happens not to be happy with it, or if he is wearing an obvious basement-bargain while everyone else is wearing fashions from upper Fifth Avenue. This "don't" works in reverse with a friend or acquaintance; with such a person it is not only permissible—it is commendable—to compliment her on her dress, if you are sincere in doing so.

3. Don't start with a *cliché*, such as the traffic problem in New York City, the difficulty of getting good domestic help, or the current newspaper headlines. Assume that the other person has read today's newspapers, and let it go at that—*unless* you can make your comment a challenge (more about that later). Once you have launched a conversation, any of these *cliché* topics may be mentioned, but they are unimaginative openers.

4. For the sake of your own social survival, don't start by saying, "You remind me so much of a cousin who lives in Del

Rio, Texas!"—or anywhere else. Everyone likes to think that he is an individual, and it is no compliment to remind him that he is runner-up to someone else—even if that someone else is a celebrity. Admittedly, I am oversensitive on this subject because I have been annoyed by such comparisons throughout my adult life. In my younger days, my "double" was a movie star whom I detested, and in recent years he has been a television detective whom I dislike even more. So, avoid the "Pardon me, but you look just like Margie" approach.

5. *Try* not to start with a question. This is not an unqualified "don't" because there are times when questions are the only things we can resort to. Use them only as a last resource. You can see from the dialogues earlier in this chapter how unproductive of any real give-and-take they can be. Sometimes they can be downright embarrassing because they give the impression that you are prying. If you have to fall back on questions as an opener, make it a rule never to ask more than *two* in succession. If you don't strike pay-dirt with your first two, sneak into another room and start talking with yourself.

By this time, you may think that I have tabooed every approach you may take to engage a stranger in conversation. Not so! Following are some suggestions for opening a conversation which you may find helpful and productive. Some of them require courage, but courage is a Sterling trademark of staunch talk. Like the steel rods that reinforce poured concrete, it makes a good foundation for building. I am listing these suggestions in the order I consider weakest to strongest—one that requires *real* courage to use.

"Do's"

1. Talk about your host (or hostess): "How long have you known Jonathon?" or "Where did you meet Peter?" These are questions, and are weak unless you can follow them up with an

amusing account of your own first encounter with your host. You must be prepared for such replies as, "I met him when he managed a bordello in Tangier," or "We were thrown into the same cell at the 66th Street 'lockup' one night when we had both been jailed for vagrancy."

2. Make a pointed observation about your surroundings. All living rooms—and most offices and restaurants—contain objects that may be used as conversation pieces. The success of this approach depends upon your being able to make a definite, intelligent observation. It should never be vague, such as, "The color scheme in this room is nice, isn't it?" (That says nothing and leads nowhere.) Try to be specific:

> a. "What beautiful lines that Queen Anne sofa has! Do you like traditional furniture, Mr. Dinkledorf?"

Mr. D. may reply that he knows nothing whatsoever about furniture styles, but don't be discouraged: You have eliminated one fruitless subject of conversation; what is more important, you have revealed yourself as a perceptive person—someone who is always respected.

> b. "Is that Mozart playing on the radio?"

Be sure that it isn't "Beat Me Daddy, Eight to the Bar!" However, if you know anything at all about music, this is fairly safe: At some point, almost any classical composer sounds like Mozart!

> c. "Why on earth does Marie have that horror of an ormolu clock on her mantel?"

No, no! When I suggested a pointed observation, I did not mean a *barbed one*. The person you are addressing probably gave Marie the ormolu clock—that's why it's there tonight! So, be careful . . .

3. Use a courtesy-gesture: "Please, take this comfortable chair by the fire," "May I offer you a cigarette?" or "Would you like me to hang your coat?" Do not overdo this; give the other person credit for being able to get around without crutches, and avoid fussing over him unnecessarily.

You can use the courtesy-gesture in reverse by asking a slight favor of the stranger: "I'm sorry, but I seem to have left my cigarette lighter at home; do you have a light?" or, "I've never smoked Slaloms; may I have one of yours, to see what they're like?" It should be a trivial favor which you ask; don't expect conversation to get off to a smooth start by trying to borrow ten dollars from a new acquaintance!

Once I shared an apartment with an advertising man who was invited to many parties; often, I was included. He used one "gimmick" again and again which falls into this category. He always wore interesting cuff-links (made from the decorations on a Samurai sword, from old Greek coins, or designed by Peruvian goldsmiths, and so on), and on our way to a gathering I would observe him slyly unfasten one of his links. Soon after he had been introduced to a lady at the gathering, he would "discover" that his cuff was undone, and politely ask the lady to fasten it for him. This trick apparently brought out the mother-instinct in the lady, and the unusual nature of the cuff-link always acted as a conversation piece. Whatever it was, that guy "made out" socially as no one else I have ever known! It was such a transparent, juvenile trick that I have never dared use it, but it *worked!*

4. Toss out a challenging statement. Earlier, I warned against using a *cliché*, such as current newspaper headlines, for opening a conversation. Let me qualify that: If you have a fresh point of view on a current topic, this can stimulate good talk. Try not to be vague ("What do you think about ....?"); instead, state your point of view:

a. I've been following closely the Heatherington case, and I am sure that he is innocent, in spite of all the circumstantial evidence. What are your views on the subject?

b. I'm concerned by the Government's announcement of [some policy]. What motivation do you suppose is behind that announcement?

In using a challenging statement as a conversation starter, it is important to remember that you are *not* doing it to win an argument. Nobody ever wins an argument; in sales jargon there is a truism, "Win an argument and lose a customer." On the other hand, you need not "pussyfoot" or "bootlick." Some of the most scintillating conversations I ever heard transpired among people who disagreed totally, but who respected the views of others.

Let us say that you express an opinion boldly, and Tim O'Connor retorts, "Oh, you're dead wrong! These are the facts [*sic*] in the matter..." and proceeds to enlighten you. What do you do?

You take Courage by one hand, and Discretion by the other, and reply, "I've always thought differently because..." (Be sure that you are *able* to state your views logically.)

Now, Mr. O'Connor is not likely to let you off the hook; he will probably proclaim that you are even *more* dead wrong, and promptly tell you why. This is the boiling point—but keep cool. Remember, you are not Abraham Lincoln, locked in deadly debate with Stephen Douglas; you are a pleasant person, trying to make social conversation with a "slob." Ease out of the situation gracefully by murmuring, "I had never thought of it in that light before; it's an interesting point of view." Then, smiling, go and ask your host for another drink. There are more than one hundred eighty million people in the U.S.A., and you do not have to get along with *all* of them!

5. Open "cold" with a humorous story. This requires a high

degree of intestinal fortitude,[1] but is such a useful way of opening other people's fund of ideas that it is worth trying. Your
story should be brief, amusing, and in good taste; above all, it
should not be one that everyone has heard. It does not have to be
a joke that has appeared in print; it is more effective to use a
personal anecdote. Use something that happened to you at work
or on vacation.

Why is this such a valuable device? If you will think of the
last time you heard a good story, you will recall that it reminded
you of (a) *another* story or (b) of something that happened to
you or your friends. This gets you and your conversation-partner
onto a definite subject, which is the gold nugget in a stream of
good talk.

I have used this story-device for many years, and—being at
heart a timid person—I must confess that I introduce it with a
little white lie to give myself courage. I search my memory for
an amusing experience, or for a story which makes some comment on human nature; then, I introduce it with, "On my way
over here, the taxicab driver told me a story which I had not
heard before. He said . . ." Or, I may start with, "Funny thing
happened at work this afternoon . . ." The white lie is that I
have not taken a taxicab to get where I am at the moment, or
that the incident I relate did not happen this afternoon—but
months ago. My conscience does not bother me too much, since
it almost always opens an animated conversation.

Only once has the story-device failed to work for me: I was
introduced to two beautiful women at a party and went immediately into what I considered a brilliant, brief and pithy anecdote, sure that it would convulse them with laughter. Neither
one of them so much as grinned; instead, the baby-blue eyes of
one of the ladies turned to ice, and her voice was knifelike as she
turned away with the comment, "I see you're one of those re-
volting little men who tell funny stories!" However, the law of

---

[1] In G.I. vernacular, "guts"!

averages will be with you, rather than against you, if you use this device.

Most of the foregoing suggestions have been mere devices. They are for the person who feels especially inadequate in social conversation. However, don't hesitate to use them if you need to. Don't be deterred by the fact that they have appeared in print; everyone will not have read this book. If you are discovered using them by someone who *has* read the book, you will have something in common, and can have a glorious time throwing verbal brickbats at it! Remember, also, that no device will substitute for polite listening, having worthwhile ideas, and expressing those ideas courteously.

Midstream

Once you have launched the ship of talk, how do you steer it? Mrs. Ramsey Hunt, one of New York City's most charming and successful hostesses, gives this advice:

> Conversation should not be like a golf game, where each player hits the same ball (if he can find it) again and again, while another player hits another ball time and again. It should be more like a tennis match, where the same ball is volleyed back and forth between the two players, or among four players, until a point is made. Who makes the point is not important; the fun of the game is in giving everyone his chance at the ball.

Carry the ball

The old chestnut, "A good listener is a good speaker," is only half true. You may listen with bated breath and shining eyes, while others talk for hours; then, when you say goodbye, the only impression you leave will be the one on the chair cushion where you sat. Take part by at least asking questions (talkers dearly love questions!), or expressing agreement or disagreement with the ideas being expressed by others.

Think of conversation as a barrel of apples; you are invited to take as many as you can carry. However, after taking an apple, do not take another until after someone else has a chance at the barrel. Participate, but do not monopolize.

Think ahead

While you are listening, try to think of a story or a comment that will fit exactly the topic being discussed. This should be fairly easy, since we *speak* at a rate of approximately 150 words per minute, while we *think* at rates between 300 and 800 words per minute. Use this differential to search your mind for some contribution.

If you do not feel qualified to talk about subjects such as international politics, Existentialism, or nuclear physics, then stay away from them. Do not go to the opposite extreme by contributing nothing more than how you arrived at the best feeding formula for your youngest child, or how John acted when he got tipsy at the country club last Saturday! There is a happy medium, and you need only to read any of the current newsmagazine weeklies in order to find it. I think it was Jacques Barzun who said that educated people talk about *ideas,* semi-educated people talk about *events,* and uneducated people talk about *people* (the current screen siren or the newest sensational singer, for example). Let the jury of your mind reflect upon Mr. Barzun's charge, and judge for yourself how often you speak like an educated person!

Stop when you're ahead

Do not try to exhaust a topic. Conversation is not a problem-solving conference, a seminar, or a workshop. When you observe one member of the group looking away furtively as if she is bored, or when you have to cudgel your brain to find something else to say on a subject, it is time for a change.

Speaking of changing the topic, let me mention one calamity that is sure to befall you if you have many conversations with versatile people. Assume that you are in the midst of an animated conversation on the subject of "jealousy." Suddenly, you think of an aphorism so pithy that it is certain to make you the hit of the evening. You withhold this little gem until you can word-polish it to a superb brilliance. Then, just as you are ready to let go with "Jealousy is always *born* with love, but it does not always *die* with it," you realize that some lowdown, conniving, son-of-a-pig has sabotaged you by changing the subject! The group is now talking about steamboats! Do you remark, "Going back to the subject of jealousy, I'd like to..."? You do *not.* Just forget your [2] little gem for the time being; there will be another occasion when you can use it. Grover C. Hall, the

---

[2] It was not yours, anyway; it was La Rochefoucauld's.

Pulitzer prizewinner, once said, "No *good* idea is lost forever." *Do not try to revive a dead topic* in conversation.

On the other hand, *do* hold on to a topic if you see that some other member of the group is utterly engrossed in it. Suppose there are five of you discussing Extra-Sensory Perception (mental telepathy). Three of the others switch to a discussion of Federal banking laws, and you can tell that the fourth person is disappointed. Then, by all means, break away from the others and continue to talk to this fourth person about telepathy. In short, do not try to revive your *own* pet topic, but be on the alert for others who wish to continue a topic they were enjoying.

Groups of five or more people tend to break into smaller groups during conversation. Groups of three do not break up because courteous people hesitate to exclude the third person: When groups of four break into two tête-à-têtes, they soon become self-conscious about their neglect of the other two, and rejoin them. When a group exceeds four, however, the old bromide of "safety in numbers" reverses, and the group breaks up. This breakup often affords you an opportunity for a courtesy-gesture: Turn to the person who has not contributed at all to the larger group, and try to engage him in talk. If his reticence to join the large group has been shyness or timidity, he will appreciate your concern for him.

Why be a "shrinking violet"?

Interject yourself and your interests into a conversation. You do not have to be "pushy" or overaggressive in order to do this. Suppose you have just asked a stranger about his profession or occupation; after he has responded, you have only to remark, "That's quite different from my work," or, "That's somewhat similar to my occupation." If he isn't a blithering idiot, he will follow this lead by asking you to tell him more. You can take advantage of a lull in the conversation to relate a curiosity-provoking incident connected with your occupation. From there, you can move on to any topic on which you have a firm footing. When you have left a group of strangers, they should know *more* about you than the mere fact that you *were* with them. Beware, however, of "taking too many apples." We can forgive others who bore us, but we can never forgive others who show that we bore them.[3]

Why be a thistle?

Try not to introduce controversial topics too early at a social gathering. Wait until you feel you have some insight into the personalities present, or until you have established some degree of *rapport* with them. As I have said earlier, never be afraid to express your convictions on a controversial issue—but *politely,* please!

Somebody needs you

Give "Lonely Lillian" a lift. In a lively conversation, there is one meek little mouse who sits in a corner and says nothing. Do not wait until her silence becomes depressing; you can include her with no more effort than the question, "What's your opinion on this?" or, "Do you approve of John's solution?" Good conversation need not go at machine-gun speed—silences are often golden and relaxing—but all those present should be encouraged to join in. Strictly speaking, this is the responsibility of your host, but it is equally your responsibility as a guest to be considerate of all present.

If "Lonely Lillian" appears so dull and unattractive that you hesitate to talk with her, reason with yourself thus: "If she has lived to grow up without getting drowned in the bathtub, or run down by a taxicab, she must have a *little* gumption, so I'll give it a try." You may be pleasantly surprised!

You need not overburden yourself with responsibility for others, because some people are not worth your time. Observe

[3] Again, La Rochefoucauld's.

people at the next large gathering you attend: You are certain to see one or two—perhaps several—standing alone, holding a glass or cup and looking utterly miserable, or wearing a frozen smile but making no human contact, and making no attempt at alleviating the loneliness of others. Their isolation is largely a result of self-centeredness. At a recent holiday party, given by an actress, I encountered such a person. She had been sitting near a doorway, clutching an empty glass and a woebegone expression for at least half an hour, so I sauntered over.

"Can I get you a fresh drink?" I asked.

"No thanks," she replied, as if she didn't mean it.

"My name is Hugh Fellows. What is yours?"

"Ellen."

"Are you in the theatre, Ellen?"

"Why do you want to know?" she countered sullenly.

"I don't, really. I don't give a damn!" I answered, as I moved over to a congenial group nearby. Some people should never be allowed out of their kennels, but they are the *exceptions*, rather than the rule.

"Hello and Goodbye"

Here are a few "parting shots" on random topics:

Remembering names

When you are introduced to someone, why don't you remember his name? The reason is probably threefold: (a) The name is mumbled by the person making the presentation, (b) you are so occupied with looking over the stranger that you don't catch the name, or (c) you just don't *care!*

If you don't catch a stranger's name when being introduced, ask him to repeat it then and there. This is far less embarrassing than calling him "Er—uh" all evening. Once you are sure you have caught the name, spell it mentally and then take another look at him to associate the name with the person. Use his name the first two or three times you address him: "Mr. Supinsky, did you attend the Community Concert this afternoon?" ... "No, Mr. Supinsky, I rather enjoyed his playing." You will not forget his name easily if you do this. I am as guilty as the next one when it comes to forgetting names, but I have proved to myself that they *can* be remembered. On several occasions, by concentrating on the matter, I have startled entire gatherings by rattling off the names of a dozen or more people present as I started to say goodbye. Yes, I'm an exhibitionist!

Making introductions

You know, of course, that the gentleman is always presented to the lady, and that a young person is always presented to an older one, except when the gentleman or the young person is of rare distinction. This, however, is not enough. If you can do it gracefully, you should give *each* person a little of the *other's* background:

> "Miss Randolph, may I present Mr. Houston? ... Phyllis is food editor for *McSwain's Magazine*, Pat. Phyllis, Pat is an attorney who specializes in copyrights."

If you are hesitant about giving the background in the presence of your two guests, you can brief each of your guests on others who will be present at the time you invite them. This may lead to disastrous confusion, if your guest-list is large, so reserve this device for small gatherings.

If your gathering consists of more than a dozen people, do not introduce a newcomer to everyone at once. Instead, present him to two or three people and leave him with them. After he has had a few minutes in which to get acquainted, ask the group to excuse him and present him to another group. You do not need to be constantly pushing and shoving your guests from one group to another, but you should take the initiative in seeing that they mix with one another. If a stranger meets half a dozen people during the course of a party, that is sufficient. Knowing your guests and their interests, you should be able to associate the ones more likely to be congenial with one another.

MOVE GUEST ABOUT <u>GENTLY</u>!

Large parties

If you are giving a large party, do not line up chairs in a semicircle around the walls of the room; this is deadly for your guests, since it allows them no mobility. Arrange your seating in clusters of three or four.

If you do not have the space to do it *properly*, then do not give large parties. My personal opinion is that there should be a special ordinance forbidding groups larger than a baker's dozen. This means entertaining more often than if you try to repay all your social obligations at once, but it also means more enjoyment for all your guests. A psychologist friend of mine entertains people at dinner about twice each week; her parties are immensely successful, and she arranges them like this: She usually invites five people—three of them are people who already know one another; the other two are strangers to the first three. In this way, she accomplishes two things: (a) The strangers find an atmosphere of friendly warmth already engendered by three friends who are at complete ease with each other, and (b) the three friends are provided with the stimulus of meeting someone new. This particular hostess declares that no intelligent private party should include more than ten guests, and I am inclined to agree with her. After all, if you want to be in a crowd, you can go to a baseball game—or take a bus ride during the rush hour!

Chapter Seven

The "Demon-Goddess," Telephone

Your Telephone Personality

AS familiar as we are with this everyday instrument, the telephone has one characteristic that is both surprising and startling: Most people's personalities *change* when they talk over the telephone—or, at least, they seem to. This is because the telephone equipment does not reproduce their voices exactly as they would sound face to face, and because we tend to assay the personality of another by his appearance as well as his voice. Thus, a person with a gruff voice which sounds chronically angry over the telephone might give quite a different impression if we could see his cherubic, smiling face and boyish haircut; similarly, one with a well-modulated, resonant voice over the telephone might take on an entirely different aspect if we could see his shifty, suspicious eyes and snarling mouth. Here is one man's experience with this personality change:

I was engaged to teach an evening class at a large university. I met the Dean and his assistant, and was told that a Miss King would take care of such things as mimeographing, making appointments with students, getting necessary equipment for use in class, and so on. I didn't meet Miss King for months, but talked with her several times a week by telephone: She had a pleasant, bell-like tone, with a smile in her voice, a friendly manner and a breezy personality. After a few weeks, I had a complete mental image of her: small, pert, efficient without being hurried, very feminine; she preferred tailored clothes—always with a feminine touch, such as a silk scarf or a corsage; she had soft, light brown hair with a windblown cut, and sparkling blue eyes. This picture was so entrenched in my mind that when I finally met her in person I was nearly prostrate from the shock. She was a hippopotamus! Her weight was close to 300 pounds, and she had great, bulging, black eyes with heavy drooping lids. After I had had a few weeks to observe her in person I realized that she was petty, suspicious of everyone, selfish and a real hellion to her subordinates.

Was the person described in the paragraph above "two-faced" —a Dr. Jekyll and Mr. Hyde? Not necessarily; most of her work consisted of dealing with people by telephone, she had been trained to be pleasant and considerate over that instrument; she *had* to be personable when dealing with outsiders in order to hold her job. But, when she had the upper hand in her own office, she didn't have to be anything except what she was.

The fact is that most of us are either more aggressive or meeker over the telephone than we are in face-to-face situations. I have tape-recorded hundreds of business and professional men and women as they attempted to solve problems or handle situations over the telephone, and in almost every case the person gave a more-than-somewhat different impression from the one he or she gave in person. There is something about the anonymity of the telephone that encourages all of us to be our "other" selves.

WHAT'S HE REALLY LIKE?

ON THE TELEPHONE, YOUR PERSONALITY IS JUDGED BY YOUR VOICE.

So, Mr. Hyde, let your other self on the telephone be pleasant, courteous and considerate. Try to talk in a relaxed manner, don't interrupt and try not to explode. Above all, try not to fall into the trap of "taking the other person's tone." This is something that professional actors have to guard against constantly: One actor, usually the most forceful one on stage, may have a definite speech pattern; if they aren't careful, the other actors tend to imitate his same speech pattern until they have lost their own distinct personality. On the telephone, let one party get angry or excitable, and the other tends to do the same thing. Beware! If you have a grievance to air, or a complaint to make, give the person at the other end of the line the benefit of the doubt by stating your complaint as courteously and as dispassionately as possible; remember, he's apt to take *your* tone. This is corny, but I've found that when I have something which I need to complain about, I appeal to the ego of the other person with something such as, "Mr. Jones, I'm in trouble, and I wonder if you could help me?" or "Mr. Jones, I don't know whether I'm stupid in operating this machine you sold me or not, but the machine and I are having a personality clash." However, if the situation demands your getting tough, the telephone is the coward's perfect weapon; the guy at the other end can't throw his telephone at you!

There is nothing more detrimental to your telephone personality—nor more maddening to the person who has to listen to you—than the habit of vocalizing pauses. It sounds like this:

> "Well, uh . . . if I were you, I'd ah . . . think this thing over. Ah . . . it's likely that the uh . . . other person is trying to understand ah . . . what you mean, but is uh . . . distracted from uh . . . getting the message because he's ah . . . also uh . . . counting all those damned 'Uh's' and 'Ah's' you're making!"

The way to avoid this is simple: Pause, think through your entire sentence, and then say it. Before the next sentence, pause again and think it through before starting it. As you may recall from Chapter Six, you can easily do this because of the difference in the speeds of thought and speech.

A last word about your telephone personality: The final impression a listener gets is apt to be the most lasting one, so try to make it a favorable one—even if it necessarily has to be an angry one. Most telephone conversations end with a statement of courtesy, assurance, or decision. Try to see that your decision is firm and fair, your assurance of action is honest, and your courtesy-statement sincere.

Solving Problems by Telephone

Every day we communicate via telephone in attempting to solve our business and social problems; often our attempts end in one or both parties feeling confused, frustrated and angry. Why? Nine times out of ten it's because we *don't get at the problem.* Instead, we try to put all the blame on the other fellow, we strive mightily to preserve our ego, or we get sidetracked on trivial or irrelevant matters. As you listen, or as you plan your telephone conversation, ask yourself, "What is the *real* problem?" If, instead of giving your opinion as to what it is, you ask the other party involved to help you discover what the real problem is, you may go a long way toward solving it. Here are some typical problems that are often handled by telephone:

The "I'm just mad!" situation

You are the personnel manager for the Trans-City Bus Company. Your company has been trying to educate the citizens who ride your buses to ask for their transfers at the time they pay their fare (indeed, there are signs in the front of all buses stating that no transfers will be issued except at the time the fare is paid), but neither the drivers nor the public have observed this regulation strictly. You have also been trying to educate your bus drivers to be more courteous to the public.

You receive a call from a Mr. Sturgis. He tells you that, beset by many personal problems, he forgot to ask for a transfer while boarding a bus this morning; later, when he went to the front of the bus to ask the driver for a transfer, the driver—No. 551—not only refused, but was downright abusive. He used profanity and embarrassed Mr. Sturgis, claiming that Sturgis had got onto the bus with a transfer and was simply trying to cadge a free ride, that Sturgis was interfering with his driving by coming up and talking to him, and so forth.

Now, if you try to defend the driver, if you try to justify the driver's action by referring to the regulation concerning the time transfers are to be issued—even if you offer to refund Sturgis the extra fare he had to pay because the driver refused him a transfer—you're in trouble. Doing any of these things can prolong the argument to ten or fifteen minutes. Your best recourse is to hear Sturgis out, without interruption, and then say something like:

"I can certainly understand your being angry, Mr. Sturgis, and I'm glad you went to the trouble of calling me. None of our passengers is going to be treated that way if we can help it! We've been doing our best to try to drill some courtesy into our drivers, but we aren't always successful. Now, if you'll give me that driver's number, I'll give him a good, stiff reprimand, and I think it's a safe bet that he'll think before he speaks next time."

And you're through with Mr. Sturgis in about two minutes.

The breach of etiquette situation

A friend has invited you to a dinner party where a distinguished statesman is to be the guest of honor. She explains that, since her dining table is small, she can invite only a few choice friends. You have kept the dinner in mind for *next week*, and were away from your office all yesterday afternoon. Today, when you look at your appointment book, you realize that the dinner party was *last night!* You call to apologize.

In a situation like this, don't look for an excuse that will justify your oversight; don't claim that the baby fell from a second-floor window, that you were called out of town suddenly on urgent business, or that your prize heifer had the colic and you had to rush her to the veterinarian. Just tell the truth, apologize, and promise that it won't happen again. (And it probably won't, because she isn't likely to invite you again!) Don't try to atone for your sins by inviting her out to dinner (she's still peeved), but send flowers or chocolates a few days later.

Let's put the shoe on the other foot: If you are the host in such a situation and the delinquent guest calls to apologize, don't give him hell. Accept his apology with good grace, express regret that he missed such a stimulating party (you can rub this in a little!), and say that you're sure you might have done the same thing if you had a lot of matters on your mind. If the invited guest who didn't show up is almost *indispensable* as good company, the next time you invite him telephone a "reminder" the day before the party. If he isn't indispensable, forget him!—but do it graciously. You must remember that human beings are human beings, and as such, are subject to human frailties. Any of us is apt to slip on a banana peel because we aren't looking at the sidewalk.

Handling complaints

When a customer calls a business firm to complain about some real or fancied injury, or about unsatisfactory goods or service, he has only two things in mind:

1. Something is wrong!
2. What are you going to do about it?

The business firm, on the other hand, has to consider three things:

1. Something is apparently wrong.

2. Who is at fault—my firm, the customer, or a third party (a carrier, for instance)?

3. How can the situation be handled in order to satisfy the customer, keep the customer, and lose the least possible money for my firm?

There are times when the customer is obviously at fault, yet the business firm will accede to the customer's request in order to retain his patronage:

> You are in charge of complaints and adjustments at Bimbel's Department Store. You receive a call from Mr. I. B. Slewfoot. He tells you that he has been trading with Bimbel's for ten years, and has had a charge account there for the past seven years. Last week, he came into Bimbel's to buy a pair of shoes. The shoe department did not have exactly what he wanted, but the shoe salesman, Mr. Triped, talked him into buying a pair of brogans which Slewfoot didn't really like, but which Triped said were the newest style. Slewfoot wore the shoes for three days and they hurt his feet unbearably. Yesterday he returned to Bimbel's and asked Mr. Triped if anything could be done about the shoes—an exchange or refund. Triped was most rude, said that the shoes could not be exchanged because it was unlawful to sell used wearing apparel as new, and hinted that Slewfoot was a habitual merchandise-swapper.

Even though you know that Triped is a fine shoe-fitter and a kind, courteous gentleman, don't try to defend his conduct. You may ask Mr. Slewfoot to give the shoes a few more days to "break in" properly; then, if they are still unsatisfactory, to bring the shoes to you (*not* to Triped—perish the thought!), and you will gladly arrange an exchange, or credit his account with the full amount he has paid for the shoes. Bimbel's is going to take a loss, but what is the price of a pair of shoes compared to keeping a customer of ten years' standing?

When the customer is at fault, and you decide to say "yes" to him,

1. Say "yes" right away, as soon as you have ascertained all the facts. (This may involve asking the complainant to allow you to call him back.)

2. Explain, clearly and fairly, what the real circumstances were and why you are granting his request. For example, Bimbel's does not make a practice of allowing customers to return shoes that have been worn; Bimbel's is willing to take a loss because Slewfoot is an old customer and friend and thinks he was unduly persuaded to buy this style of shoe.

3. Look forward to many years of serving the customer happily (in other words, hope for future business).

The customer is *not* always right, and sometimes it is necessary to say "no" to his request for an adjustment of his complaint. *Life* magazine reports a ludicrous example of this:

> It is illegal to sell alcoholic beverages in the State of Mississippi. Nevertheless, they are sold there to the tune of about $1,450,000 worth each year. The State authorities know it, and turn their backs on the sale, *except to exact a State tax* of 75¢ for each case of illegal wine and $4.20 for each case of illegal whisky sold within the Mississippi borders. Acting under orders from Governor James Coleman, the Mississippi National Guard once seized a $20,000 shipment of liquor and smashed every bottle of it. The owner of the shipment had already paid the State tax on it, and applied to the tax collector for a refund of his tax money. His request was denied by the tax collector, who told him, "That's just one of the hazards of your occupation. After all, the black market tax is not a license to sell." [1]

When the customer is at fault and you must refuse his request, it has to be done with great tact if you are to retain his

[1] Norman Ritter, "A Tax on Lawbreakers Only," *Life*, May 11, 1962, p. 11.

good will and—what is more important—his trade. Here are a a few hints on how to say "no" tactfully:

1. Explain clearly the facts in the case.
2. Appeal to the customer's sense of fair play and justice.
3. Say "no" courteously, explaining that your policy is to protect him from high prices quite as much as to prevent losses to your firm.
4. Express hope that this little incident will not affect your future happy relations.

When your business firm is obviously at fault, you always grant the customer's request for an adjustment. Even saying "yes," however, can lose a customer for you if you do not explain how the injury occurred and assure him that it is not likely to occur again. Here is a suggested procedure in granting a request for reparation:

1. First, tell the customer what adjustment is being made. This is what he wants most to hear.
2. Explain how the mistake occurred, and appeal to his humanity in understanding that people *do* make mistakes.
3. Tell him what steps you have taken to see that it will not happen again.
4. Express sympathy for his inconvenience, and hope for happy business relations in the future.

Often you are called by a customer complaining about something that is not really the fault of your company; it may be the fault of a carrier to whom you have entrusted shipment, or a firm to whom you have subcontracted work. It is, nonetheless, your responsibility to follow through and try to get a satisfactory adjustment for the customer. Assure him that you will investigate the matter for him and will call him back at the earliest possible moment. Be sure that you *do*. When you have finished your investigation and are ready to call the customer, here is a safe procedure to follow:

1. Thank the customer for past business and express sympathy for his present inconvenience.

2. Tell him what steps you have taken in order to get an adjustment from the party at fault.

3. Assure the customer that the party at fault has a past record of reliability; this affects the prestige of *your firm* in doing business with this third party. Never castigate the third party.

4. Reassure the customer that he is not likely to be inconvenienced again.

To summarize briefly how you should handle problem situations over the telephone:

1. Listen carefully. If the complainant is angry, don't interrupt him until he has finished.

2. Try to be earnestly helpful. Don't let the offended person think that you take his injury lightly or are trying to "brush him off."

3. Get at the problem, and don't be sidetracked by minor issues or personal prejudice.

4. Never argue—instead, act!

Telephone Selling

First, let me distinguish between telephone solicitation and telephone salesmanship. I am so firmly opposed to blank solicitation by telephone that I cannot be objective about it; to me it is not only an annoyance, but also a criminal invasion of privacy. Whenever I stop whatever I am doing to answer my home telephone, and a strange voice starts a sales pitch, I cut him off with a short speech that is so savage and insulting that it would do justice to a mulcskinner or a riverboat boatswain. Imagine what your home life would be like if everyone in your home town who had something to sell rang your telephone only once a year!

Selling is always more effective when done in person. However, your telephone may aid you in selling if you use it in the following ways:

1. You may call a prospect (on his *business* phone, please!) to ask for an appointment.

2. Having presented your product to him in person, you may call him to inform him of an additional feature or service offered by your product. Many salesmen purposely omit some feature of their product in their first presentation, so that they have an excuse to telephone their prospect about it later; this jogs the prospect's memory, and keeps him thinking about the product. You should limit the number of features to one or two.

3. You may telephone to ask for a decision, when a reasonable time has elapsed after your first presentation.

4. If you have sold your product to a friend of your prospect, you may call the friend and ask him to give your prospect a call, expressing his satisfaction with your product.

Whenever you use your telephone for sales purposes, always ask the person you are calling if he is free to talk for a few minutes. Most people will tell you if they are too busy to talk with you, but there are a few Milquetoasts who will suffer in silence, while their resentment at your interruption builds up; then, as they bang down the receiver, they say to themselves, "He knows what he can do with *that* product!"

Sample Problems

Here are a few problems which might conceivably be handled by telephone. After reading each one, think how you would handle it, then look at the answers which follow at the end of the chapter.

1. You are the owner of Darby's, a large furniture store in a large city. Mrs. Wren, who lives in a smaller town forty miles away, has recently built a new home and has furnished it throughout with furniture from Darby's. The Italian Renaissance dining room suite she wanted had to be ordered specially from the factory, and did not arrive until today, two weeks after promised delivery. You sent it to her, still crated, at noon today. It is now 5 P.M. (closing time), your moving truck is in a garage across town, and your driver has gone home. You are just about to leave the store when Mrs. Wren calls you. She has just returned from shopping to find the dining room suite, but it's a mess! Legs on three of the chairs are broken, one of the sideboard doors is ripped off its hinges, and there are deep scratches on the surface of the table. She is expecting thirty guests tonight at 8 P.M. for a housewarming party, and is hysterical. How would you handle her problem?

2. You are vice-president in charge of sales at Stylerite, Inc., maker of women's dresses. The Mademoiselle Dress Shop in a nearby city has ordered six dozen cotton print dresses from you, indicating that it intends to use the dresses as a "leader" in its spring sale. You have sent the Mademoiselle Shop newspaper cuts and other advertising material to use in promoting sales, and had promised delivery of the dresses one week ago. The owner of Mademoiselle telephones you that the dresses have not arrived; the sale opening is three days away and the owner has advertised the dresses. Which of the following answers would you give to the owner?

a. The dresses have not been shipped because the Mademoiselle Dress Shop is delinquent in its payment on your last shipment; you have dictated a letter to this effect this morning.

b. Owing to a strike of cutters, you have not been able to complete the order. The strike has been settled, but you have orders much larger and more important than Mademoiselle's, which you must finish first.

c. The dresses were delivered to Acme Trucking Company eight days ago to be sent to Mademoiselle.

3. Daniel's Stationery Store has been a valued customer of your firm (stationery and printing) for six years. For the past three months, however, you have not received their customary sizable monthly order. Rumor has it that Daniel's is dealing with a competitor who is probably not giving him a price advantage over you. Your boss asks you to call Mr. Daniel and ask him why his orders have not been coming in.

Some answers

"There are more ways than one to skin a cat," is an old bromide, but it is still true. You may handle the foregoing problems in many ways, so long as you consider the needs of the other person, and the urgency of the situation. However, here is one way each has been handled successfully:

1. This actually happened. Mr. Darby assured Mrs. Wren that he would reorder or have perfect repairs made on her dining room suite, and—considering the urgency of her situation—would get her a substitute suite to use tonight. He went to a nearby gas station, hired a pickup truck and a couple of neighborhood boys, selected the best looking dining room suite from his floor samples, and personally hauled it out to her. It cost his store $50, but with thirty guests coming to Mrs. Wren's party, it was worth more in word-of-mouth advertising than a full-page ad in the city's largest newspaper.

2. Most people select solution *a*. They do so because it is human frailty to put the blame on the other fellow. The choice of *a* is a poor one, and in some states the manufacturer is liable to a lawsuit for damages if he has promised delivery—no matter how much money Mademoiselle owes. The choice of *b* is a poor one also; it makes Mademoiselle seem unimportant, and no one likes to feel that way. Your best choice is *c*, and offer to follow up on the matter by calling Acme Trucking; tell Mademoiselle that you'll call back and report, and that if Acme can't get the dresses to the shop in time for the sale, you'll send a substitute lot by special truck.

3. This could be handled much better by calling on Daniel's in person. However, it was handled successfully by telephone: The caller telephoned Daniel ostensibly to tell him about a new product; he mentioned a drop in price on another item, and casually asked about Daniel's supply of a third item which Daniel had been buying in large quantity. He was pleasant and friendly; Daniel appreciated the large firm's personal interest and came back into the fold.

Part
Three

Conversation
in Public

When You
"Group-Talk"

IN these pages I have outlined briefly the format of those occasions where a group of individuals think and speak together within the framework of various structures. Details are given in other chapters in this book. This condensation, however, should tell you at a glance what sort of gathering you should organize to accomplish certain purposes.

The Convention or Meeting

Purpose

To give information on past activity (periodic reports), to vote on official business, and to plan for future activities of an organization or groups with mutual interests.

Format

The convention consists of one or more general sessions, plus face-to-face committee meetings, symposia, panels or lectures for individual interest groups. The general session is usually a peri- odic meeting, composed of voting members, with committees functioning between regular sessions. Parliamentary procedure is almost mandatory in a general session.

The Convention

The Workshop or Seminar

Purpose

The sharing of information by experts, in order to train one another in new skills and knowledge, or to devise better methods of accomplishing objectives.

Format

The workshop consists of a general session, followed by small face-to-face groups of special interests. The seminar is a face-to-face group with or without a trainer. Both may consist of more than one session.

Round Table Discussion

The Panel Discussion or Round Table

Purpose

To exchange ideas, express points of view, and discover areas of agreement or disagreement.

Format

Face-to-face group with leader. Decisions and conclusions not necessary, but areas of agreement or difference may be defined by leader. May or may not have audience.

The Conference

Purpose

To solve a problem, to formulate policy or to arbitrate.

Format

Leader and face-to-face group. Members of the group are usually from the same organization (unless purpose is arbitration), and have interest in same problem. No audience.

The Symposium

The Symposium

Purpose

To present various facets of the same subject by experts in their respective fields. This is done by a series of formal talks, rather than by discussion.

Format

Two or more speakers and chairman. Chairman introduces speakers; after all speeches have been delivered, chairman directs questions from audience to speakers.

The Forum or Debate

Purpose

To present opposing sides of an issue or question.

Format

Two or more speakers address audience. If more than two speakers, chairman introduces those of opposing opinions alternately. In forum, questions are permitted from audience; in a debate, they are not.

The Briefing Session

The Briefing Session

Purpose

To inform or instruct members of the same organization or interest group.

Format

An expert or staff of experts and group who perform similar services. The experts lecture or demonstrate; questions from group permitted during and after briefing.

Chapter Nine

The Experts Speak
(Discussion and Symposium)

TWO types of group talking which take place before an audience are the panel discussion and the symposium. Each seeks to present to listeners the thoughts and opinions of experts from one or more fields. Their value is that they present their listeners with several points of view, rather than that of only one person.

The Panel Discussion

The panel discussion (sometimes called a round table) is informal. It consists of a moderator and a small number of participants (more than five are apt to prove unwieldy). The participants talk at random, without receiving permission from the moderator. It is less likely to be as informative as the symposium because participants have not organized their material formally,

154

they are prone to digress, and they are dependent to a great degree upon the provocativeness of the questions posed by the moderator. There is rarely audience participation in a round-table discussion, although there is no reason why there should not be, provided time permits.

The panel discussion does not necessarily try to solve a problem; it need not come to any conclusion; its value is in hearing interesting people explore a subject, exchange ideas and discover areas of agreement or disagreement with one another. It should have all the spontaneity of good social conversation.

The moderator

Although any gathering of able people promises interest, provided they are willing to participate, the panel discussion's success will be determined by the moderator. A good panel discussion should interest and stimulate its listeners as well as its participants, and it will do this only if the moderator has prepared challenging questions and case histories or specific examples for the members. He should study the subject thoroughly, ask exploratory questions of experts in the field, and get opinions of experts other than those taking part in the discussion.

In preparing questions, the moderator should phrase them so that they cannot be answered simply in the affirmative or negative. For instance, "What can American industry do to meet foreign competition?" is better than "Do you think American industry should take steps to meet foreign competition?" It is even better to cite a specific example, such as, "Senator Brass-water, in a television interview last night said that our government must pass higher import tax laws immediately, must lower the amount of money Americans may spend abroad, and must reduce corporation taxes in order to meet the competition of foreign industry. What is your opinion of the Senator's statement?"

Here are a few other questions a moderator may use to "draw out" members of a discussion:

1. Can you give us a specific example of the situation you have described? Can you give us a few more details?
2. If you were faced with a problem such as [describe problem], how would you attempt to solve it?
3. What have been your experiences with ....?
4. Can you suggest other possibilities?
5. Do you mind if I ask you why you think as you do?

Before the discussion takes place, the moderator may furnish the participants with a list of some of the questions he intends to ask, so that they may give some forethought to the problem. He should hold some questions in reserve, to add spontaneity to the meeting.

While the moderator is not a chairman, and does not have to give permission for members to speak, he does try to keep the panel on the subject. Minor digressions are permitted, because they are often amusing, but the members should be enticed back to the main topic if they wander too far afield. The moderator attempts to draw out all members of the panel, just as the successful conference leader does, and he tries to squelch gently the overtalkative person by asking him to hear other members.

It is important that the moderator be absolutely fair and impartial. He should never take sides in a disagreement, although he may intervene to ask the disputants to define their terms if he thinks that the disagreement is a purely semantic one.

If the moderator knows that areas of disagreement are likely to exist among members of a discussion group, he will do well to withhold questions on those areas until he has covered matters on which they are likely to agree. This gives the members time to become at ease with one another and to acquire confidence that if a disagreement occurs, it will be handled with mutual respect. Most disagreements are on opinion—not on facts.

If one member interrupts another, the moderator may ask the interrupter to wait until the other member has finished. The moderator may, if he wishes, impose a time limit on each member in which to talk on one particular topic, but this can stultify spontaneous response. However much in love with his questions the moderator may be, if he asks one that arouses no interest and response among the members, he should drop it and not try to force a response from them.

The panel members

In organizing a panel of experts, the chairman of the affair should try to select people with varying personalities, and people whose opinions differ somewhat; this will obviate the moderator's being surrounded with a group of "yes" men.

The members of a round table discussion should give the subject some thought beforehand. In order to provide *interest* for his listeners, a panel member should come prepared with one or two specific examples or case histories which illustrate his point of view; in order to *stimulate* a lively discussion, a panel member should prepare a few challenging questions of his own.

In the chapters on conversation and conference participation, I speak of a person's right to disagree. This right should be recognized even more strongly in a round-table discussion, for differences of opinion make for lively talk. However much one disagrees with another member of the panel, one must not descend to personal sarcasm, and should make every effort to see the opposing point of view.

The panel member should try not to digress, he should not monopolize the conversation, he should not interrupt. In general, the members of a panel discussion should observe all the courtesies advised for the members of a problem-solving conference, with the added responsibility of trying to *interest* one's listeners.

The Symposium

The symposium is much more formal than the panel discussion. It is apt to be more informative, and can be extremely stimulating because the audience is usually invited to participate in a question-and-answer period. While it is no more than a series of prepared speeches on different facets of the same subject, its value has been underestimated in both business and education circles.

Format

The format of the symposium is simple. The chairman introduces a series of speakers; each speaker delivers his speech; then the chairman asks for questions from the audience for the speakers to answer. Usually there are no more than four speakers and no fewer than three. With more than four, it makes an interminably long session, if each speaker is given sufficient time to explore his subject. If there are fewer than three, the exploration of the subject tends to be shallow.

Suppose we take the somewhat trite subject of "Juvenile Delinquency" as an example. The four speakers participating might be a law enforcement officer, a psychologist or psychiatrist, a social worker and an educator. Each would discuss juvenile delinquency from his professional point of view, possibly suggesting some solution. During the question period afterwards, the chairman would direct any question dealing with emotional problems and conflicts to the psychologist, questions dealing with living conditions to the social worker, and so on. In the case of a general question on the subject, the chairman may ask which of the speakers would like to volunteer an answer; sometimes two or more members will want to comment on the question, and this is permissible.

Value

You can see that this type of speaking not only offers interest by utilizing several personalities, but also provides a wider scope of understanding of a subject or problem. Inviting the audience to ask questions, and allowing the speakers to express different points of view, gives a subject an immediacy which would be lacking in the ordinary speech.

It seems to me that here is an instrument for indoctrinating and training employees that has been neglected. How much better to give a group a coordinated indoctrination, where various departments are involved, than to indoctrinate the employee into each department separately.

In education, can you imagine how stimulating the use of the symposium-type teaching could be? Instead of teaching history, sociology, literature, art and economics separately, with each course ignoring the period of history being considered in other courses, they would be taught pretty much as one reads one's daily newspaper. A student could learn what was going on in all five areas concurrently, so that developments in those fields would be as vivid to him as if he were reading them in the daily newspaper.

Function of chairman

The chairman does not participate in delivering the content of the symposium to the listeners, but he should be thoroughly familiar with the subject. More often than not, the chairman plans the symposium and selects the speakers. When doing this, he should try to break down the over-all subject into topics which will be interesting to his audience, and should delineate carefully the area to be covered by each speaker, so that one speaker will not trespass onto another's territory.

The chairman does not interject his opinions into the symposium: He gives each speaker a *brief* introduction and announces that speaker's topic; at the end of a speech, he makes no comment except to thank the speaker; and he does not attempt to answer questions from the audience. In inviting members of the audience to ask questions, he may ask the questioners to rise when posing a question, and he may limit the number of questions to one per person (a valuable safeguard, that!). A word of warning here: The chairman must be absolutely impartial; if several people rise to ask questions, he should be careful to call upon them in the order of their rising. The chairman must maintain control, however, and has a perfect right to interrupt a member of the audience who is bent on expressing his opinion or making a speech from the floor. He simply says firmly, "I'm sorry, sir, but time does not permit us to allow speeches or opinions from the floor. If you have a *question,* I shall be happy to ask the members of the symposium to try to answer it."

When the time allotted for questions has expired, the chairman must be firm. It is common practice for him to warn the audience that he can entertain only one or two more questions before the allotted time expires. Then, he thanks the speakers once again for their coverage of the subject and their willingness to answer questions, thanks the audience for their challenging questions, and says goodnight. The chairman's greatest temptation is the same as that of a conference leader: He tends to want to participate too actively, instead of performing his proper function.

Function of members

It need not be said, except for emphasis, that you should try to make a good speech if you are on a symposium. You must confine yourself strictly within the amount of time you are allotted for your original speech, if you are not to irritate the chairman and audience and antagonize other members of the symposium. When a symposium is a part of a larger program—at a convention, for example—this is particularly important because of limitation of time and availability of space. You should also restrict your talk to the area assigned to you. If you have any doubt as to whether you are doing this, contact the chairman and ask if you are infringing on another speaker's territory. In answering questions, try not to evade an issue; if you feel that you are not qualified to answer the question authoritatively, ask for the opinion of other symposium members. If a member of the symposium expresses an opinion with which you disagree, start an argument *only* if your professional integrity is at stake.

Several years ago, I was called at the last minute to substitute on a symposium on speech courses in adult education at the National Convention of Speech Association of America. I protested that I could not possibly write a paper [1] at that late date, but remembered that I had a paper on speech curricula for business and professional people which I had written for a seminar five years previously when working for my Ph.D. I could dust it off, add a few interesting anecdotes and use it; some of the thoughts in it were original and—I egotistically thought—valuable, so I agreed to take part in the symposium.

I arrived at the city where the convention was being held only a few minutes before I was supposed to take part in the symposium, so I was introduced hastily to the other speakers and we took our places on the platform. The first speaker, Professor X, was introduced and launched a lengthy explanation about what methodology he had used in preparing his paper, how he had validated his findings, *et cetera*. I thought, "How deadly dull *this* is going to be!" and started thinking of something else.

Then, like the sting of soap in one's eyes, I realized that he was reading from my own paper, *verbatim!* I opened my manuscript and followed him, word for word, for more than two pages; when he finished, I had not one single finding which I could present. My initial shock was followed by anger, for he

---

[1] If this is a snide remark, I'm glad! Speech teachers, at speech conventions, rarely make speeches; they *read papers* instead, and most of them are dull as mud!

gave me no credit for the material he used, nor did he give any recognition to the university for which the curriculum was designed. Such rank plagiarism was unpardonable in a supposedly ethical academician. I hesitated to start a fracas on the platform before an audience of perhaps a hundred colleagues, but I was determined to expose the theft. So, when I was called upon to speak, I rose, tore from my manuscript the two pages which Professor X had read, and handed them across the table to the offender.

"Professor X has already read two pages of my paper,[2] and since the plans he outlined have been used for the past five years in my university, suppose we talk informally about how they have worked out in practice." Professor X turned scarlet with discomfiture, the audience howled with laughter, and we had a very lively question-and-answer period. If your integrity is at stake, defend it, but do so with *aplomb*.

[2] I recalled later having mailed a carbon to some student from another university who was doing research on adult education; the student turned out to be Professor X!

The Problem-Solving Conference

THERE is no more valuable, useful group speech activity than a properly operating conference. You will note that I did not say "properly conducted" conference, although the leader is important. A properly operating conference is one in which a number of people place their brains at the disposal of a *problem*—not at the disposal of a person. A conference can do the following far better than an individual can: solve problems, make sound decisions, forestall future mistakes and secure active cooperation from subordinates. In order to do these things effectively, it must be a *conference*, and not something else masquerading under that name.

The purpose of a true conference should be to solve a problem. This may involve formulating policy, determining future action, organizing and distributing authority or responsibility, or extricating one's firm from a difficult position; its single purpose is still the solution of a problem. If the purpose of a meeting is anything other than this, it is not a true conference. In order to find out what it is, consult Chapter Eight.

Why Conferences Fail

Now that we have a clean-cut idea of what a conference is, why do so many of them fail? There are many reasons, but from observations over many years, I believe these to be the chief reasons for failure:

"Passing the buck"

A conference is often used as a substitute for weak administration. When an administrator feels inadequate to make routine decisions, he often confers with others to get a joint decision; then if the decision proves to be a mistake, he has someone with whom to share the blame for making it.

Enforcing decisions already made

The conference is sometimes used as a persuasive tool; i.e., an attempt to force a decision *already made* upon subordinates. The leader and a few of his cohorts have reached a decision which they know will be objectionable to other factions in an organization; nonetheless, they believe that if they can get the members of the opposing factions into a conference the leaders can either win them over or make it *seem* that the opposing faction members have agreed to the decision.

Size

Keep your conferring groups small. Democracy may be the safest and fairest manner of accomplishing something, but it is also the slowest and most wasteful. If the problem to be solved involves twenty-four people, you will progress faster if you hold three conferences of eight members each *before* getting the entire group together. In the initial stage of problem-solving, too many cooks may spoil the broth.

Poor timing

If you are notified of a conference that is to take place **three** weeks from today, you will make a notation of it on your calendar and forget all about it for three weeks—minus one day. Too short a notice is just as bad; it gives one no time for preparation. A conference should be called (a) short enough in advance to give it a sense of urgency and (b) far enough in advance to allow participants to gather materials and make some preparation.

Preparation

Conferences fail because of lack of preparation—both on the part of the conference leader and on the part of the participants. Closely allied to this is the lack of *methodology* on the part of the leader. He may meet his group with an agenda in mind (or written out), but years of experience on the part of successful conference leaders have proved that there is one format that is almost *always* successful; too many leaders ignore it, or are unaware of it.

The Ideal Format

A conference should benefit by the thinking of several minds, and there is a method by which this can be accomplished. I have chosen to explain this method from the position of the conference leader—*not* to exaggerate his importance—because it makes the explanation a little more active. There are four steps in a well-conducted conference; suppose we call them "The Four D's":

Definition

This is the only step in the conference where the conference leader does a considerable amount of talking. After thanking other members of the conference for participating, he restates the problem to be solved, and defines any terms whose meanings may be doubtful, so that everyone has an equal understanding of the manner in which the terms are to be used. He may need to give some of the background of the problem—perhaps the causes leading up to the present situation to be discussed. If it seems to be required, he may stress the importance of the solution to the problem at hand, or the urgency of an early decision. At this stage, he may call for any special materials which he has asked other members to prepare (sales figures, accident reports, floor-space requirements, cost accounts, and so forth) to give the entire group a fuller understanding of the problem. When he has done this, he should *shut up*, except in the instances cited below.

Discussion

This is the "drawing out" period, wherein the conferees explore the problem and attempt to solve it. Some of the methods they may use are explained in this chapter. It is during this period that the conference leader must avoid the temptation to talk too much; he is present to draw out *other* people. If he does his job well, he will have little time for active participation, for it is during the discussion that he should perform three tasks:

1. He tries to keep the discussion limited to the issue being considered, and to prevent needless digressions.

2. He encourages the reticent members to contribute, and "squelches" the member who tries to monopolize the discussion.

3. He makes notes, in a condensed form, of all major contributions.

The discussion in a smoothly running conference should be primarily among the members of the group, rather than a series of questions and answers between the leader and individual members. (See Chart B.) Remember, this is a conference, not an inquisition!

POOR   GOOD

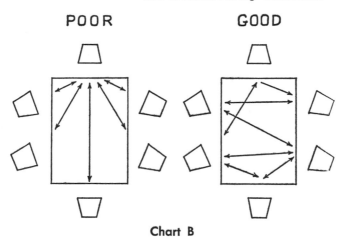

Chart B

Decision

As the group progresses toward a solution of the problem, the leader assists them by trying to put their solution into words satisfactory to all. If he has listened intently, he may recognize that they are nearer to a solution than they realize; this is only one of the reasons the leader tries to maintain absolute objectivity. When the group has come to its final decision, the leader writes it out and reads it to them for their corrections and amendments.

Diplomacy

Even though the problem has been solved to the satisfaction of those concerned, there is still another step in a successful conference. This is a diplomatic gesture by the leader, acknowledging the contributions made by the conferees. No doubt, during the attempt to reach a solution, some members have made suggestions that were not usable; these suggestions should be acknowledged, with sincere thanks. They may have stimulated some other member of the conference to think of a more feasible suggestion, and they *were* a sincere attempt to help. If all donors are thanked, they will be more willing to work their brains at the next conference.

The Conference Leader

The cautious, overdeliberative thinker does not make the best conference leader; nor does the impetuous, impatient person. The best leader is one who can listen without impatience, who can think objectively, who can exercise enough authority to prevent useless digressions, and who has enough of a sense of urgency to press gently for a solution. It is unfortunate, but almost inevitable, that the conference leader is almost always someone who outranks the other participants. This can cause the conferees to hesitate to disagree, and often to be reticent in speaking out. An Air Force Colonel whom I know overcomes this handicap in this manner:

> All my command's problems are solved by the conference method, and by lower echelon and noncommissioned officers without deference to rank more than any adult should pay to any other adult who is working with him on a problem. When my men come in for a conference, I tell them, "Gentlemen, these insignia on my uniform do *not* denote intelligence—only responsibility. *You* have the intelligence about this problem because you're closer to it than I; so, if you solve the problem, I'll take the responsibility." It works every time.

I have mentioned before the necessity of the conference leader's keeping the conferees on the immediate issue. There are two occasions when the leader will *deliberately* digress from the problem for good reason. One is when two or more conferees get into a heated argument and the disagreement is becoming a matter of personal ego; at that point the leader may interject an irrelevant matter to allow the disputants a short while to "cool off." Another is when the conference has been going on for an unusually long period of time; then the leader may introduce a bit of humor, or some sort of digression. When the participants are given a little relief from cudgelling their brains, they can tackle the problem again with fresh minds. Here are some other suggestions for the conference leader:

Encouraging the silent member

You may try an occasional question such as "What do *you* think of that suggestion, John?" or, "Let's get John's reaction to that proposal, shall we?" However, if you, as the conference leader, know beforehand that John is apt to be shy and reticent, you should call upon John *first*, just after you have made your opening statements. Shy people tend to recede more and more into the background as other, more talkative people carry the burden of the conference; however, once John has made a contribution, he has an investment in the conference, and he is apt to protect that investment by continuing to contribute.

"Squelching" the monopolist

On most occasions the overtalkative person who threatens to monopolize the conference can be subdued by saying something as simple as, "That's a good idea, Pete, but I wonder if we may hear what the others think? What about you, John?" However, if you get one of those self-appointed, bellicose "big shots," who thinks that nobody's ideas except his own are worthwhile, you may have to play rough. First, interrupt him to ask that he clarify or explain something he has said; then, in the midst of his explanation, ask him to explain something there; if necessary, ask him to explain something in his explanation of his explanation of his original explanation! [1] In this way, you can so "befuzzle" him that he will be delighted to shut up and sit down. Now, you must make amends for hurting his ego (after all, his monopoly

---

[1] If you want to start a "knock-down-and-drag-out" scrap with your wife (or husband), try this the next time she or he explains something to you.

of the conference *may* have been only enthusiasm!), so you ask him a simple question which he can answer with a "yes" or "no." The chances are that he will answer in the affirmative or negative, and think awhile before he launches again into a filibuster.

Recording progress

Earlier, I said that the conference leader should take notes of all major contributions. Why not have a stenographer take down everything that is said? Because it involves a tremendous waste of time. In looking over her transcript, you will have to wade through a morass of words to get at the *meat*. There is a much more efficient way: If the conference leader will take notes intelligently, he can do a much better—and more concise—job than most stenographers. Here's how: Prepare for yourself a number of large sheets of paper, numbered consecutively, and divided into equal spaces for each conference participant, with the participant's name in one square. (See Chart C.) Suppose Fred makes a proposal; while he is wording it, you can condense it and write it down in the square bearing his name.[2] Now, Al objects to the proposal; you condense Al's objection and write your condensation in Al's square, drawing a line from one to the other. Tom makes a counter-proposal; that is condensed and entered in his space. Joe adds something to Tom's proposal; this is entered, and a line connects the two. You can see that you may soon have a page of what looks to be spaghetti, so—when page one begins to get crowded, you go on to page two. When the conference is over, you will have a complete condensation of all the major contributions to it. If you have numbered them, you can repeat them in sequence. This procedure requires a little practice for it to work well, but it is worth the effort.

---

[2] This can be done easily because of the difference between the speed of speech and the speed of thought. How often have you surmised what a person was going to say when he was no more than halfway through a sentence?

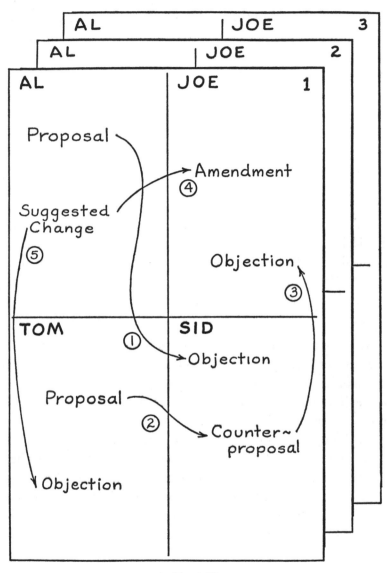

Chart C

Time limit

Stay strictly within the time limit allotted for the conference. If the problem has not been solved within the time limit, close the conference and call another at a later date. Tom has probably promised his wife that he would pick her up at the hairdresser's; Al had planned to catch the 5:40 train; Joe has promised that he would trim the hedge on the front of his house before dinner; when the conference runs overtime, their minds will be on other things. So, unless there is a dire emergency, adjourn.

Mutual respect

When people get together to work on a problem, there should be an atmosphere of common respect and consideration. Not only should the conference leader respect the other members of the conference group, but he should try to maintain respect for one another among the conferees. All should remember that each participant in a good conference has four rights:

1. The right to be recognized (as himself and as a member of whatever group he belongs to—the personnel department, the safety office, and so on).

2. The right to be heard (even if the leader needs to prod him occasionally to speak up).

3. The right to disagree—with *anybody.*

4. The right to "stick his neck out" without getting his head chopped off. Nobody ever makes a "stupid" suggestion in an earnest conference ... even if it is somewhat impractical. (There have been times when an impractical suggestion has stimulated another to think of a valuable and highly practical idea.)

The Conference Participants

Too much has been written elsewhere about conference leadership, and not nearly enough about conference *participation.*

This overemphasis reached its zenith for me several years ago, when I received a book for examination entitled *How to Win the Conference!* [3] Now, if anyone goes into a problem-solving conference with the intention of *winning* it, it is not a conference but a struggle for power. However, members of a conferring body *should* have some knowledge of the conference leader's duties, so that they may assist him ably.

Perhaps the most important things for a participant to remember are those four "rights" listed at the end of the preceding section. You must respect the other man's opinion and his right to take a fair share of time in talking. Here are a few other hints that will help you in becoming an effective problem-solver in a conference.

Reflective thinking

Prepare yourself for the conference by doing some creative thinking beforehand. I don't mean letting your mind wander vaguely over the general subject of the conference; try to find *your* solution to the problem. If you will cultivate the habit of thinking in a definite pattern—such as in the following outline— you will find it useful in helping you to arrive at a solution. Ask yourself these questions:

1. What is the problem, and how did it arise?
2. What are the possible solutions to the problem?
3. Which of the possible solutions is most practicable because of
    a. Its effect on management and personnel?
    b. Its effect on customers and stockholders?
    c. Its cost, and effect on future expansion?
4. How can this solution be put into operation?

James Harvey Robinson, in his interesting book *The Mind in the Making* [4] claims that we spend the bulk of our free time in

---

[3] Publisher's and author's names omitted to spare them embarrassment.
[4] New York: Harper and Brothers, pp. 33-62.

aimless reverie and daydreaming, a large portion of it in making routine personal decisions (most of them trivial in nature) and justifying those decisions or blaming ourselves for having made them, and precious little time in disciplined, constructive thinking. He is probably right. So, stop your daydreaming—and think!

Preparation

Ask yourself what documents and materials, accessible to you, might be useful in the conference. Don't wait until you are asked to find them and bring them into the conference room; get them and study them beforehand. If necessary, copy the pertinent parts so that they will be easy for other members to read. Nothing helps a conference achieve what it sets out to do more than *exact* information—sales records, accident reports, survey results, statements of profit and loss, and so forth.

Flexibility

Don't fall so much in love with your own idea of how the problem should be solved that you refuse to listen to others. Although your solution may not be acceptable, it could inspire other participants to find one that is. So, be willing to compromise, unless you feel that compromise is actually and definitely detrimental to the successful solution of the problem.

Self-discipline

Contribute to the talk whenever you have something to contribute, but don't monopolize the conference because others are less talkative than you are. Resolve to stick to the issue, and to help the leader by "spreading around the talk" among others. Avoid anger in replying to personal remarks, and avoid the temptation to sulk when you find your ideas are not esteemed as highly by others as they are by you. Remember, two heads are better than one *only* if they are working *together*.

One final word: In order to become proficient in solving problems with a group, you need experience. Much of value can be gained by observation, if you have the opportunity to visit conferences as they are held by other people. This chapter should have given you some of the reasons why a conference fails or succeeds; watching others in conference will teach you something about your own conduct in a group trying to solve a problem.

Chapter Eleven

"Let's Call
a Meeting"

WHETHER or not you belong permanently to an organization which holds regular meetings, you will almost surely, at some time, have to take part in a meeting or preside over one. To be able to preside or participate in a meeting with knowledge of how it should be conducted is an asset. This chapter contains information which will enable you to participate or preside with equal assurance.

Club Organization

The officers required in a club vary according to the needs and purposes of the club itself. On page 181 I have charted the officers usually found in a general club organization. Some of them may be dispensed with; you may need to add others. Here we will discuss briefly some of the major officers with a brief outline of their duties.

Presiding officer

The president of an organization usually acts as chairman of all meetings, except committee meetings. In his absence, the vice-president takes the chair, and in the absence of the vice-president, the secretary, the treasurer, the parliamentarian and the sergeant-at-arms, in that order. This order really depends upon the bylaws.

The chairman must be a person of tact, firmness and impartiality. While, as a member in good standing, he may vote on any motion brought before the assembly, he does not usually do so. As referee between any two opposing factions, his impartiality is difficult to sustain if he has voted consistently with one or the other. In case of a tie vote, the Chair exercises its voting privilege to break the tie.

If the chairman wishes to discuss or debate a motion, he asks some other member to take the chair and preside while he is discussing the motion. Impartiality!

The chairman should have a basic working knowledge of parliamentary procedure, and should have at hand at all times a copy of the constitution and bylaws of the organization and a chart indicating precedence of motions. He must insist that the club entertain only one main motion at a time. He must be patient with fools and tactful with tyrants. If he has not committed it to memory, he should have before him the club's permanent order of business. (See pages 180-182).

While the president of an organization usually officiates at all public occasions, he may appoint a toastmaster to serve in his stead. If empowered to do so by his constitution, the president may appoint committees, subject to appeal by the members. His chief duty, however, is to conduct the meetings in an orderly manner and to get things done. Here are a few pointers on form and conduct in meeting.

1. Always refer to yourself as "the Chair," not as "I".

2. Refer to each speaker by name. If you do not know his (or her) name, ask, "Will the member please state his name?"

3. Keep at hand a list of the committees, so that you may refer to their personnel by name.

4. Restate each motion clearly and loudly, so that all will know what is under consideration.

5. Announce the results of each motion clearly: "Carried!" or "Lost!"

6. Keep business moving by avoiding useless voting. If the group apparently is in complete harmony on a motion, simply say, "It has been moved that the club send flowers to the widow of Robert Donavan; if there are no objections, flowers will be sent. (Pause for discussion) It is so ordered."

The secretary

For this hardest-working position in an organization, someone should be chosen for his ability, rather than his personality or popularity. Unless your club has a parliamentarian, or a president who is an authority on parliamentary law, the secretary should be thoroughly conversant with its rules. He (or she) should be able to take notes rapidly, and be able to read his own writing after it gets cold! He should be able to read aloud correspondence to the club, or records of business, in a loud, clear voice, and to preside over the meeting if necessary.

After each meeting, the secretary puts his minutes into final form, for approval or amendment at the next meeting. The minutes should include:

1. Name of club, presiding officer, date and place of meeting, and type of meeting (regular or special).

Example: The Old-Timers Club of St. Petersburg, with President Octo Genarian presiding, met in special session on Friday, May 13th, 1963, 2:30 P.M. in the Ageless Antique Shop.

2. All formal actions of the club, and all main motions and their disposal.

> *Example:* The minutes of the previous meeting were read and approved as corrected.
>
> The motion to have a shuffleboard contest with the Misogamist Club, postponed at the May 1st meeting, was carried after being amended to read that the contest be held on the Dotage Shuffleboard Courts.
>
> It was moved by President Ab Origines, seconded and carried, that the Chair appoint a committee of three to investigate the cost of purchasing six wheel chairs to be kept in the foyer of the civic auditorium. The President appointed Lon Gevity, C. Nility and Grey Crutch for this committee.

When the minutes are approved, this should be noted ("Approved as read" or "Approved as corrected"), signed by the secretary, and usually countersigned by the president.

The secretary keeps on hand a copy of the constitution, bylaws and all documents of the club. He keeps handy a roster of all members, and calls the roll when required. At the beginning of each meeting, he presents the chairman with the order of business of that day (what business is outstanding, what special orders must be taken up, what committees are to report, and so on); at the end of each meeting, he provides the chairman of each committee with a list of his committee members and any special instructions ordered by the club for that committee.

In addition to all the above duties, the secretary handles all official correspondence of the club. If correspondence is heavy, it is usually assigned to a corresponding secretary.

Committees

Standing committees are those which function over a long period of time, usually from one election to another. Temporary committees are those which cease to exist when they have accomplished their purpose. Under "Standing" one might list membership, scholarship, program, and publications committees; under "Temporary" one might list nominating, fund-raising (for a special period), investigating and special campaign committees.

Committees are generally appointed by the chairman or president, since electing a group of people to a committee is cumbersome and time-consuming. However, if your bylaws stipulate, or if members insist, that committees be elected, I suggest that you use a limited voting procedure. Let us say that a committee is to be elected: Each member votes for only *one* candidate; the results are likely to be that the majority of members will elect three of the five committee members, but the minority will at least be represented by having elected the remaining two. (See Chart D.)

Order of Business

While the order of business in an organization is traditional, it should remain flexible within the bounds of parliamentary law and your club's bylaws. All standing committees do not necessarily report at every meeting; the treasurer may report only every quarter, and the nominating committee only when an election is imminent. When possible, the presiding officer and the secretary should confer *prior* to a meeting to decide the agenda; they should keep in mind, however, that they are not allowed to alter the Order of the Day without the consent of the membership.

Because of a special program made available to us only at this meeting, the Chair proposes that the Club dispense with reports from committees at this meeting. Are there any objections? (Pause for objections; there are none.) It is so ordered.

CLUB OR SOCIETY ORGANIZATION CHART

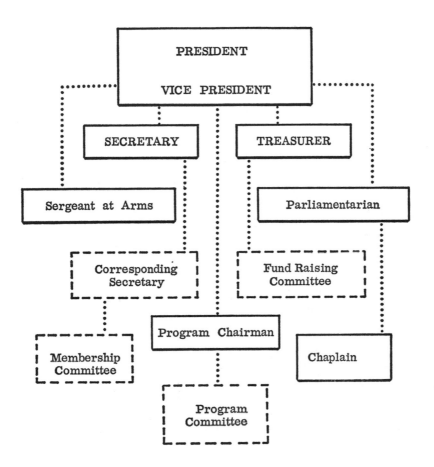

Other committees, if size and activities of club warrant:

Elections, Nominating, Publications, Legal, Investigating,

Charity, etc.

Chart D

Below are two formats for the order of business in a meeting; they are more detailed than is necessary in most meetings. The steps marked with an asterisk (*) are often *not* a part of the order of business in a meeting.

Format of business meeting without program

1. Call to order.
*2. Invocation (if opening prayer is customary).
*3. Roll call (if customary, or if it is questionable whether a quorum [1] is present).
4. Reading of minutes, and their approval or amendment.
*5. Appointment of *pro tem* officials vital to the meeting if regular officials are absent (acting secretary, sergeant-at-arms, parliamentarian, and so forth).
6. Reports of committees or officers (if due), or special orders.
7. Old business.
8. New business.
9. Announcements.
10. Adjournment.

Format of meeting with program

1. Call to order.
2. Minutes (may be dispensed with, except for special orders, which require two-thirds vote to dispense with).
3. Very urgent business—new or old.
4. Program.
5. Announcements.
6. Adjournment.

---

[1] A quorum is the minimum number of members who must be present to transact business legally. It is usually fixed in a club's bylaws at a certain percentage of the total membership. If a quorum is not present, the club may *discuss* any issues at question, but may not *decide* any such issues.

Parliamentary Procedure

Most of us hesitate to act as chairman of a meeting or as president of a club because of that old bugaboo, parliamentary procedure. At first glance, it seems a cumbersome and complicated process; indeed in all its fine points as practiced by the United States Congress and the British Parliament, it is an onerous subject. However, for a presiding official of the average club or meeting, knowing a few principles, and having at hand a good reference on parliamentary procedure [2] are all he needs. Study of these few principles is well worth the effort when one remembers the *purpose* of parliamentary procedure, which is to insure that (a) all minorities receive a fair hearing, (b) that the majority rules, as in any democratic process, and (c) that the group can accomplish its business without being blocked by any one or two tyrannical, powerful members. For purposes of a simple study of the subject, I have divided parliamentary procedure into three general headings: Nominations, Motions and Precedence.

Nominations

Nominations are best made by a committee—either elected or appointed—so that possible candidates can be considered carefully. This committee may submit one or more names for the post to be filled, depending upon the size of the organization. To protect the group as a whole against the nominating committee's prejudice in favor of a candidate who would not really be the choice of the majority, the chairman almost always calls for nominations from the floor.

If you use a nominating committee:

CHAIR: You have heard the report of the nominating committee. Are there any further nominations from the floor?

2 Some references are listed at the end of this chapter.

HENRY: Mr. Chairman!

CHAIR: Mr. Henry? [It is not necessary to use the lengthy "The Chair recognizes Mr. Henry" except in extremely formal organizations, or when there is some dispute as to who has the floor.]

HENRY: I move that the nominations be closed.

GEORGE: Mr. Chairman! (*Chair recognizes him.*) I second that motion.

CHAIR (*Ignores the motion in order to give others a chance to speak.*): Are there any further nominations? (*Long pause; there are no further nominations.*) It has been moved and seconded that nominations be closed. All those in favor signify by saying "Aye" ... Opposed, "No."

If you do not use a nominating committee:

CHAIR: Nominations are now open for the office of Treasurer.

PETER: Mr. Chairman!

CHAIR: Mr. Peter?

PETER: I nominate Mr. Aaron Burr for Treasurer. [Nominations do *not* need to be seconded; one or more members may second the nomination to show their approval, but it is a waste of time.]

CHAIR: Mr. Aaron Burr is nominated. Any further nominations?

GEORGE: Mr. Chairman!

CHAIR: Mr. George?

GEORGE: I nominate Alexander Hamilton for the office of Treasurer.

CHAIR: Mr. Alexander Hamilton is nominated. Any further nominations?

PATRICK: Mr. Chairman!

CHAIR: Mr. Patrick?

PATRICK: I moved that the nominations be closed.

PETER: I second that motion.

CHAIR: It has been moved and seconded that nominations be closed (etc.).

Whenever there are *two or more* candidates, the move to close the nominations must be moved, seconded and passed by a two-thirds majority of those present (a quorum, as specified in your club's bylaws).

Voting should be by ballot, to obviate personal friction. If your club is very informal, however, the candidates may be asked to withdraw, or simply to close their eyes, and votes may be taken by a silent show of hands. The number of votes required for election is usually specified in your bylaws; it is usually a simple majority of those present if they constitute a quorum.

The move to suspend the rules and elect by acclamation is in order only if your constitution permits, when the majority of the membership is clearly in favor of a candidate and there is no overt opposition. To elect by acclamation usually requires a three-fourths vote.

Motions

The actual transaction of business in a meeting is relatively simple: (a) A member proposes an action, (b) another member seconds the proposal, (c) the group is given an opportunity to discuss or debate it, and (d) a vote is taken, whereby the proposal is either accepted or rejected. At any point before or during the discussion, a member may propose that the debate be limited or extended, that the original proposal be "tabled" (that is, postponed indefinitely, or to another meeting), or that it be divided or amended. Most such proposals must be seconded by another member. However, if a member has knowledge that a certain proposal will cause hurt, undue friction, or be obnoxious or insulting if discussed, he may interrupt the meeting without being recognized by the Chair and object to the motion's being considered. The Chair then takes a vote on whether or not the motion will be considered. If two-thirds of those present vote *not* to consider the motion, the matter is dropped without further ado, and may not be brought up again at that meeting. Let's see, using a ludicrous example, how this works:

"Rat Court"

MICKEY: Mr. Chairman! (*He is recognized by the Chair.*) I move that we put a warning bell on the cat and chop off its tail.

DOR: Mr. Chairman! (*Is recognized.*) I second that motion.

CHAIR: It has been moved and seconded that we put a warning bell on the cat and chop off its tail. The floor is open for discussion.

FIELD (*rising, and thinking of* MRS. TABBY, *who is present, and a member of the club*): I object to consideration of this motion!

CHAIR: There is objection to the consideration of this motion. Those in favor of considering it say, "Aye." (*There is a great chorus of "Ayes."*) Those opposed, say "No." (*There are two "No's"*—MR. FIELD MOUSE's *squeak and* MRS. TABBY's *meow.*) The "Aye's" have it by more than a two-thirds vote, and the motion will be considered. Is there any discussion on the motion that we bell the cat and chop off its tail?

FIELD: Mr. Chairman! (*Is recognized.*) I move that we amend the motion by preceding the word "cat" by "Tom," and substitute the word "his" for "its," thus having the motion read, "We will put a bell on the *Tom* cat and chop off *his* tail."

MRS. TABBY (*thinking only of herself*): Mr. Chairman! (*Is recognized.*) I second that motion.

WHARF: Mr. Chairman! (*Is recognized.*) I move that we lay this motion on the table indefinitely.

CHAIR: You are out of order, Mr. Rat. After a two-thirds majority has voted to consider a motion, it may not be tabled without some discussion. The discussion does not have to be lengthy.

WHARF: I accede to your point of order, Mr. Chairman, and move that debate on this motion be limited to ten minutes.

MICKEY: Mr. Chairman, I second that motion.

CHAIR: It has been moved and seconded that debate on the pending motion be limited to ten minutes. Those in favor, say "Aye." (*The motion is carried.*) The "Ayes" have it by a two-thirds vote, and the motion to limit debate to ten minutes is carried. Discussion is now on the motion to bell the cat and chop off its tail.

MRS. TABBY: Mr. Chairman, I rise to a point of order!

CHAIR: State your point of order.

MRS. TABBY: An amendment to the main motion has been moved and seconded; that amendment must be discussed and voted on before we may discuss and vote on the main motion.

CHAIR: Your point is well taken. Thank you. Is there any discussion on the motion to amend the pending motion to have it read, "to bell the Tom cat and chop off his tail"?

WHARF: Question! Question! [That means he is calling for a vote; he is eager to see Tom shackled! He could also say, "I move the previous question" or "I call for a vote."]

CHAIR: A vote has been called for. Is there any further discussion?

TIT: Mr. Chairman! (*Is recognized.*) I call for a division of the motion.

CHAIR: You are out of order, Mr. Titmouse. We are voting on an amendment to a main motion. You may enter your motion to divide the question *after* the amendment has been carried or lost. All in favor of the amendment say, "Aye." (*The amendment is passed.*) We are ready to entertain further discussion of the main motion which now reads "We will bell the Tom cat and chop off his tail."

TIT: Mr. Chairman! (*Is recognized.*) I call for a division of the question. While I am anxious to have *all* cats belled (*a withering look at* MRS. TABBY), to warn us of their approach, I object to the chopping of their tails, and wish *that* part of the question to be voted on separately. I'm sure that many of us feel that this is a cruel act of mutilation that is not in keeping with our own desires to maintain our bodies intact. I move that the question be divided.

MICKEY: Mr. Chairman! (*Is recognized.*) I second Mr. Titmouse's motion.

MRS. TABBY: Mr. Chairman! (*Is recognized.*) I object to the division. Everyone knows that Tom is a dirty old philanderer who has been unfaithful to me with every pussy in town. Furthermore, he's a vicious mouser! (*Piously*) Now, I never *touch* a mouse unless we have expelled him from the Club, but Tom . . . ! Putting a bell on Tom would be useless unless his tail is chopped off, because that old scalawag can move so stealthily that you might never hear a tinkle of the bell; however, he could never be *sure* of catching a mouse without the balance which his *tail* gives him!

DOR: Mr. Chairman, I suggest that Mrs. Tabby has ulterior motives for not wanting the question divided. First of all, I question her good faith in joining the Mouse Malefactors Society; next, I suggest that she wants to see Tom mangled because she is jealous, and there is always the chance that he will be destroyed in the process, which would leave her free to . . .

WHARF: Mr. Chairman, I rise to a point of order!

CHAIR: What is your point of order?

WHARF: Mr. Dormouse spoke without being recognized by the Chair. Furthermore, the aspersions he cast upon a fellow member in good standing are most indelicate and unbecoming and . . .

DOR: Mr. Chairman, I rise to a question of privilege!

CHAIR: Please state your question.

DOR: I request that Mrs. Tabby come down from that rafter on which she is crouching, and from which she could pounce upon any of us without a second's warning!

CHAIR: Your privilege is granted. Will Mrs. Tabby please resume her place in this assembly?

(MRS. TABBY complies. MR. DORMOUSE *is ruled out of order and apologizes. The division of the question is voted upon and carried, and the main motion, now reading only "to bell the cat," is voted upon and carried.*)

MRS. TABBY: Mr. Chairman! (*Is recognized.*) I move that Mr. Dormouse and Mr. Wharf Rat be appointed to bell the cat.

DOR: Mr. Chairman! (*Is recognized.*) I move that we adjourn!

WHARF: Mr. Chairman! (*Is recognized.*) I second that motion!

CHAIR: It is moved and seconded that we adjourn. Those in favor of adjournment say, "Aye." (*The motion is carried!*)

Here are a few things to remember about main motions: A motion is not in order if any other motion is pending. The previous motion must be voted upon, tabled, or voted out of consideration before a new motion may be made. If a motion is complicated, it should be written out, so that members can study it, step by step. Very often a complicated motion is divided and voted upon piecemeal. Once carried or lost, a main motion cannot be taken up again at the same meeting.

Precedence

There are certain laws, or "fixed" motions that exist in parliamentary procedure. They take a rigid priority, one over another. Many of them have been illustrated in the episode about belling the cat. They are used to *block* undesirable transaction of business as well as to expedite business fairly. While this book's scope does not permit listing these in detail, they can be found in most of the books cited at the end of this chapter. A list of these motions, in order of their precedence, and with indications as to whether they require seconding, majority or two-thirds vote in order to be carried, should be kept by the secretary at all meetings, as a handy reference. The tyro chairman should also keep a list before him until he is thoroughly familiar with the more common motions and their order of precedence.

Book list

Here is a list of books that go into more detail on parliamentary procedure and on conducting meetings.

Davidson, Henry A., *Handbook of Parliamentary Procedure*. New York: The Ronald Press Company, 1955.

Jones, O. Garfield, *Parliamentary Procedure at a Glance*. New York: Appleton-Century-Crofts, 1949.

Robert, Henry M., *Robert's Rules of Order*. New York: Scott, Foresman & Co., 1951.

Simmons, Harry, *How to Run a Club*. New York: Harper & Bros., 1955.

Sturgis, Alice F., *Learning Parliamentary Procedure*. New York: McGraw-Hill Book Co., 1953.

Chapter Twelve

Selling
an Idea

ALL talking is persuasive speaking in a very broad sense: You persuade listeners of your sincerity and respect for them; you persuade listeners that you know what you're talking about; or you persuade listeners that you are friendly and are happy to be among them. However, there are some occasions when your primary purpose is to change the thinking of your listeners or to move them to some course of action. How can this be done? In this chapter we shall explore some of the means whereby people are moved to think and act as they do.

Attention and Interest

You cannot persuade people unless you can arouse their interest in your subject; you cannot arouse their interest unless you get their attention. Now, there is a difference between attention and interest: If you are interested in color photography, you will attend a lecture by an expert on that subject and *give* him your attention, because your interest is there already. If, on the other hand, you are dragged to a lecture on trade agreements between the United States and Canada—a subject about which you may be totally unconcerned—the speaker must *arouse* your interest if he is to get a favorable response from you. In order to do this, he must get and hold your attention.

During the depth of the financial depression of the early 1930's, a large New York newspaper carried out this experiment:

It sent two of its reporters to stand on the edge of a sidewalk in Times Square; one of the reporters was given an automatic computer and was told to count all the people who passed by; the other reporter was given $100 in ten-dollar bills, and was told to stand silently holding out one of the bills in front of him. If any passer-by stopped to question him—or make any remark whatsoever—the reporter was instructed to tell the stranger that he could have the ten-dollar bill if he would promise not to tell anyone. The newspaper was really giving away $100, but it took nearly eighteen hours to get rid of it (and this was during the depression!), while more than 7,000 people—many of them hungry, no doubt—passed by.

"The passers-by weren't paying attention," you may say. Oh, yes they were! There is no such thing as a vacuum in attention. But they were paying attention to their own personal matters; the two reporters did nothing to divert that attention to the ten-dollar bill.

As you enter an office to make a sale, or take your place at a conference table, your listener—or listeners—surmise instantly: "He's going to be dull [or interesting]; he's intelligent [or stupid]; he's a good guy [or he beats his wife]." Then they start thinking of their own personal affairs unless you do something to get their attention and hold it. Whether they give their attention to the doodles they are drawing or to your ideas depends on *you*.

A student told me this story: Nine-year-old Sammy's father fell asleep in church and started snoring. A neighbor nudged the boy and whispered, "Sammy, wake up your father." With perfect equilibrium the youngster replied, "The preacher put him to sleep; let *him* wake father up!"

Attention With Purpose

Any fool can attract attention. If a gentleman dressed in a conservative business suit wears a huge pink ostrich plume in his Homburg hat, he will attract attention; if a sedately dressed lady wears one bright red stocking and one bright blue one, she will attract attention. Getting attention is not enough; what counts is focussing that attention on the points you make to accomplish your purpose. How can it be done?

Humor

During a conversation on the state of the American theatre, the late Brander Matthews told this story:

An unsuccessful young playwright became so desperate that he contemplated suicide. He sat on a bench in Central Park and tried to decide between hurling himself from the top of a skyscraper or turning on the gas in his kitchen. A woman from a much older profession came along and sat down beside him.

"What's the matter, bub—down and out?" she asked.

He nodded glumly and she consoled, "Aw, come on kid; keep ya chin up! What's ya racket?"

"I'm a playwright."

"Ya mean ya write plays—for the *theeayter?*" she asked.

"I write plays. . . . Nobody buys them."

"Tough!"

Both sat disconsolately for a few moments; then the woman roused herself, turned to the playwright and proclaimed, "Do ya know what's wrong with your racket—and with mine? They both been ruined by *amateurs!*"

The story was most appropriate, for the point that Professor Matthews wanted to make was that the numerous "little theatre" groups that had sprung up throughout the country had become a substitute for the older, professional stock and touring theatrical companies.

Humor is always a good way of getting and holding attention —*if it is relevant*. However, to tell a funny story just to "put your listeners in a good mood," can actually lose their attention unless it makes a point. Here's why: If you can remember the last funny story you heard, you will recall that it reminded you of (a) another funny story or (b) something that happened to you or someone else; an irrelevant story or remark may start your listener's attention wandering away from the point you want to make and you'll have to lasso him with a rope to drag it back.

Curiosity

You can get a listener's attention if you can arouse his curiosity in your idea or product. In a conference on how to improve management-labor relations, the leader started the discussion by holding out one closed hand and stating, "Gentlemen, I hold in my hand something which no human eye has ever seen." He opened his hand and revealed a peanut which he shelled, dropping the two kernels onto the conference table.

"Neither I nor any other man had ever *seen* those kernels inside this peanut shell, but I had faith that they were there," he continued. "If management and labor are to solve their problems with amity and justice, they must have faith in each other's good intentions." He made his point and got attention at the same time.

Note how the following titles of magazine articles are worded to create curiosity:

"I Came Back From the Dead" (*Maclean's*, October 8, 1960).

"The Texan Who Conquered Russia" (*Reader's Digest*, August, 1958).

"Hark the Shrieking Angels!" (*The Bulletin*, December, 1959).

"The Case of the Faceless Spy" (*This Week*, October 23, 1960).

"The Mink's in the Sink" (*Reader's Digest*, April, 1962).

"Can Machines Replace Teachers?" (*Saturday Evening Post*, September 24, 1960).

Questions

Some salesmen use the device of asking a question as an opener. When they do, they try to phrase a question which the prospect will answer in the affirmative. When public speakers or panel moderators open with a question, they try to find one that creates curiosity or that is challenging. Personally, I feel that advertising copywriters have overworked this device to the point of nausea; for example:

Are you tired? Nervous? Overworked? Headache-y? Run down? Do you wake up every morning dreading the day ahead of you? If so, take PLENACOL! Plenacol has the secret ingredient X-5 ...

Oh, spare your listeners that! Still, a fresh and provocative question is a good way to open a speech or sales talk.

Quotations

The use of an apt quotation is an effective method of getting attention. The leader of a symposium on teen-age problems opened the symposium by stating, "There is an old French proverb which says, 'Old men give good advice when they can no longer set bad examples.' " It was particularly appropriate for the occasion. If you use a quotation, it should be fresh—not one that has been bandied about until it has become trite. There are many excellent sources of apt quotations, among them the famous *Bartlett's Familiar Quotations* (now not so "familiar"), the section of "Quotable Quotes" in *The Reader's Digest*, the occasional page of quotations in *The Saturday Review*, and an occasional column of quotations in *The New York Times Magazine*. Don't overlook *The Holy Bible* and the works of Shakespeare.

Motivation

When you have your listener's attention, what is the next step in selling an idea? You must show that your subject is of importance to him. In other words, you arouse his interest. *Who* and *what* usually interests people?

People

People are interested in themselves—sometimes a regrettable fact, but a fact nonetheless. After themselves, they are interested in their family; after their family, they are interested in their friends; after friends, acquaintances; after acquaintances, people in their community; after the community, people in their state or section of the country; after those, people in their country as a whole. Most people do not really care about the rest of the world, unless what is happening out there is likely to affect them, their family, friends and so on, in diminishing degree.

The headlines of your local newspaper scream that an earthquake has killed 2,000 people in Patagonia. "Whew!" you whistle; "that's getting rid of them in a hurry." Then you callously turn the pages to the sports section, the stock market reports or the comic strips. At the bottom of one column is a short "filler" which reads:

> John Dinkeldorfer, of 3240 Oyster Avenue, Gateville, broke his leg last night while trying to enter his home through the cellar when he found that he had lost his key. He is in Cedrus Hospital.

"Hey, Molly!" you call to your wife. "Old John Dinkeldorfer broke his leg last night in his own cellar. I'll bet the old boy was drunk."

"Oh, I don't think Mr. Dinkeldorfer is a heavy drinker," your wife protests.

"Well, I'll bet he didn't get that red nose of his from a sunburn," you opine.

You and your wife may spend five minutes talking about one man's broken leg, while 2,000 Patagonians lie dead on the front page. Why? Because Mr. Dinkeldorfer lives just down the street from you.

I am not suggesting that all people are cruel or heartless; it is simply a fact that we are more interested in those who are the nearest to us. Our natural interest in people is like a target. In selling an idea, try to show your listener that it gets as close to the center of the target as possible.

The Four L's

Now *what* interests people? What motivates them to do what they do? Psychologists list as many as thirty motivating forces; however, most people act as they do because of one of four stimuli—or a combination of two or more of these four. To help you recall them easily, I have named them "The Four L's:"

> Life
> Love
> Laurels
> Liberality

Life

This is man's instinct for self-preservation—his desire for security of food, clothing, and shelter from the elements and his enemies. You can sell the average American male anything if he believes it will make him healthier or prolong his life. This basic drive no doubt accounts for the tremendous sales of vitamin products in this country. Most Americans have access to enough nutritious food to make dietary supplements unnecessary; still, they gulp down millions of dollars worth of vitamins every year. I myself take them!

Sometimes we do not admit the strength of this drive. A friend told me this story:

> In Germany, toward the end of World War II, the truck in which I was riding exploded a land mine and was blown to bits. When I regained consciousness, I was hanging upside down from the limb of a tree by a chain that had been lying loose in the truck; it had freakishly wrapped one end around my leg and the other end around the tree limb twenty feet away. Everyone else was killed, and I had several broken bones and severe cuts and burns. I knew I was going to die, and I think I would have except for my mother. You see, she is an orphan and a widow, so I am her

only living relative. I knew that if I allowed myself to die, it would literally kill her. So I hung on to life for *her* sake.

As tender and as touching as his sentiment was, it was nonsense; he stayed alive because *he didn't want to die!* Notice how the following excerpts from magazine articles—and even their titles—appeal to this instinct for self-preservation:

> Kenny Weldon had been a pitiful bag of bones . . . when he first came to the clinic. On therapeutic vitamins . . . he is 223 pounds of bone and muscle, looking not more than 50 though he is 61 . . . "What saved our lives?" he roared. "The vitamins, the food, the good Lord—and Dr. Spies." [1]

> Remember, the safest place for smooth tires is the ashcan. If you insist on squeezing the last dollar's worth of mileage out of them, then keep your life insurance paid up! [2]

> Timely check-ups against disease, and simple precautions against accidents to the eyes, are worth more than the finest medical skill that can be obtained after accident or disease has occurred. [3]

Try to show your listener that the idea you are selling will promote his safety, health or well-being. If you can do this you can arouse his interest and satisfy his attitude of "Why should I listen to you?"

Love

By this "L" we designate man's second strongest primitive drive—the sex urge. This drive involves much more than the accomplishment of an orgasm or the getting of children; it is also the stimulus for creativity. Sublimated, it is responsible for

[1] Paul de Kruif, " 'The Vitamins, the Food—and Dr. Spies,' " *Reader's Digest,* September, 1958.

[2] Paul Kearney, "Tired Tires Can Kill You," *Traffic Safety,* August, 1958.

[3] John K. Lagemann, "Facts and Non-Facts About Eye Care," *Redbook Magazine,* May, 1960.

many of our masterpieces of painting, sculpture, music, literature and even philanthropy. It is given added impetus by the primal self-preservation instinct in this way: A man does not feel that he is lost to the world irretrievably if he leaves behind something that bears his stamp—a child, be it of body or of brain. Even without this added impetus, it is a strong drive; you can sell almost anything to the average American woman if she thinks that it will make her more attractive to the opposite sex; that is why "fashion" is one of our country's largest industries. Notice how this drive underlies the following quotations:

I am a woman—hence my chief interest is men.[4]

Anxious mothers, fretting because their daughters are not "popular," prod, coax, fatten, slim down their immature girl-children, much as fight trainers groom their protégés for a bout.[5]

After reviewing a good many of the books available on this subject, I have come to the conclusion that . . . the mistake the sex manuals make is that they overemphasize the physical factors and fail to emphasize the emotional factors.[6]

If you can show your listener that what you have to sell will have a favorable effect on his sex life, his emotional satisfaction, or his creativity, you have him half-sold already.

Laurels

People want to be thought well of; they want prestige. This "L" denotes the basic primitive drive of ego satisfaction. You can do almost anything to a man—beat him physically, lie to him, steal from him—and he may forgive you if you make restitution and give time for the wound to heal. There is one thing,

[4] Cleo Dawson, "How to Manage a Woman," *The Rotarian*, September, 1957.

[5] Lucille G. Lakes, "Where Are the Ugly Ducklings?" *McCall's* Magazine, September, 1960.

[6] Dr. David R. Mace, "What the Sex Manuals Don't Tell You," *McCall's* Magazine, January, 1958.

however, which you can never do to him unless you want to make him your enemy for life: *You must not make him ridiculous in the presence of his fellow men.* Circumstances may force him to work with you and be superficially pleasant to you, but he will never forgive you if you have really hurt his ego. To paraphrase Hamlet, he will smile and smile and be a villain still. In the following example, note how strongly the person telling the story was affected by an ego-hurt. This is an actual transcript of a tape recording lent me by a psychiatrist; names, of course, are fictitious:

> When I was in the seventh grade, this guy came to our school to coach athletics and teach science. His name was Tom Richards, and he must have been a sadist, because he surely made me miserable for two years. He was a big guy, about six feet two. I was small, and I guess, by his standards, I was somewhat effeminate because I liked music and dramatics, I grew flowers and I did oil painting. I was also manager of the basketball team which Richards coached, and he made my life hell. I would come into the locker room and he would say, "Cover yourselves, men; here comes 'Miss' Brubaker." In science class, or in study hall, if I looked up from my books, he'd come out with something like, "Brubaker, is that a Gloria Swanson or a Norma Talmadge pose?" I hated his guts!
>
> Well, I worked my way through college and then through graduate school, and I taught for the State University for two years before going into business for myself. One semester the University sent me into the backwoods of the state to teach an extension course which all public school teachers were required to pass in order to hold their teaching licenses. On the very front row sat Tom Richards! In all those years he had never got his B.A. degree; you could get a teaching license in those days after two years of college, but you had to continue to take courses in order to hold it. He had a family and could not afford to go back to college full-time. His work was as good as some of the others in the class—maybe better—but I flunked him. He lost his license. I still feel guilty about it.

My psychiatrist friend assures me that this testimony is from a kind, philanthropic man of high achievement. His youthful ego-hurt was so great that it caused him to lose objectivity and take a petty revenge.

Vance Packard in his book *The Status Seekers* shows to what ridiculous extremes people will go to preserve their ego; obviously, not everyone is so ego-conscious, but this drive does play an important role in motivating people in general. Note how the following advertising slogans appeal to the ego of their readers (the italics are mine):

> "For the look of *leadership* . . . the Centurian Suit by *Society* Brand."
>
> "POWER . . . in the palm of your hand . . . *Power* to make full use of all *your ability*—not just a part of it."
>
> "Cadillac . . . *universal symbol* of *achievement.*" [How small— or big—is the Universe?]
>
> "How *executives* unwind in Puerto Rico: Golf 52 weeks a year."
>
> "*Important people* . . . come to the Caribe Hilton."
>
> "It's *stylish* to drink Irish."
>
> "*Men of Distinction* drink Calvert's."

Convince your listener that the idea you are selling will increase his status, ability or prestige, and there's a good chance that he will buy it.

Liberality

This "L" encompasses a liberal point of view, understanding the desires of others, and a willingness to promote the welfare of others—in short, altruism. It is an acquired drive, rather than a basic, primitive one, but it is a strong motivating force in the Western world. (Any New Yorker who has to ride the subways during rush hours will swear that there is not an iota of concern for the welfare of others in that seething, clawing, shoving, jostling mass of animal bodies!) Yet it exists—if not in the New York subway—at least in other parts of our country, as the following excerpts show:

> Phelps Memorial's Woman's Hospital Auxiliary boasts about 1,000 active members, one third of whom, working in the hospital last year, gave 41,350 hours of time. . . . Most of the volunteers are busy housewives who have their own families to look after. Some arrive by Cadillacs, others by bus. . . . The thing they have in common is the urge to do something useful for the community hospital. "The surest way to discourage the auxiliaries into staying home," said one administrator, "is not to give them too much to do but to give them too little." [7]

> For the last 30 years a tough, saturnine little man named Elias Nour has been operating a one-man rescue service for persons trapped on the treacherous slopes of Georgia's Stone Mountain, 15 miles from Atlanta. In that time the mountain has claimed 7 victims. But Nour has saved 34 others [in addition to 6 dogs]— perhaps a record for mountain rescues made by one man. He has performed this service without pay. [8]

Altruism gets a boost from both ego-preservation and self-preservation. From ego come such sentences as, "Mention my name to the manager of the Plaza Hotel, and you'll get special treatment; he's an old friend of mine," or, "Tell Pete Johnson I sent you to his store and he'll give you a special discount." From self-interests come statements such as "I'm willing to pay more taxes to be sure that my child's school is free of fire hazards," or, "Those poor, starving war orphans! What if it were my child? I'll send ten dollars to CARE." The last statement is based on the superstition in the Western world that whatever endangers a large number of others may eventually threaten us.

[7] Paul Kearney, "Salute to the Ladies in Pink," *The Modern Hospital*, February, 1958.

[8] Hugh Park, "The Unsung Hero of Stone Mountain," *The Reader's Digest*, September, 1958.

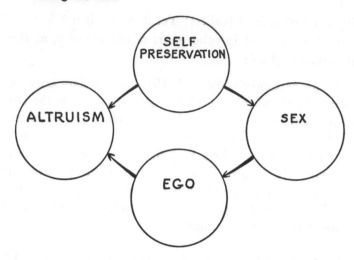

Although altruism in its pure form is a genuine concern for the welfare of others, it exercises a strong force on those who are genuinely selfish. If a person is genuinely "hog-selfish," he knows it and feels guilty about it; consequently, he will empty his pockets—in public—to prove that he isn't!

Each of the four "L's" is a strong motivating force in itself. Most of the time, however, there are two or more of them at work, causing a person to think and act as he does.

Other motivating forces

There are two other strong factors that enter into decisions made by your listeners. These are (a) the desire for change and its opposite, (b) the desire to remain static. These forces work primarily with different age groups. The unexplored, the unknown or the "brand-new" appeal to younger people, and they are more apt to respond to a plea for change than are older people. Older people are more content to muddle along with conditions as they are, provided those conditions are not *too* unpleasant; they take the position of "Don't rock the boat!"

In summary, if you can convince your listeners that what you have to say will contribute to their health or well-being, their emotional security and creativity, their status and prestige, or their desire to contribute to the welfare of others, you will surely generate interest in what you have to say.

Impact

Once you have captured the attention of your listener and have aroused his interest in the idea you are trying to sell, how can you be sure he will *remember* what you have said? (Obviously, if he doesn't remember, he will not react to your message.) Suppose we try an experiment to demonstrate why people remember some things and do *not* remember others. Now, please follow directions carefully: On page 206 you will find three word lists. Cover Word Lists #2 and #3, and read Word List #1 *aloud* slowly, allowing about one second between speaking each word. Read the list *only once*. After you have read it, close the book and write as many of the words as you can recall within the space of one minute. Now, do the same with Word Lists #2 and #3. Remember, read each list *aloud* and read it *only once*. Don't give yourself more than one minute to recall the words on each list.

Now, check the words you recalled against the lists in the book. Here are the likely results:

Lists #1 and #2: You probably recalled between six and eight of the words in List #1. This is average for adults, when a list of ten words has no strong association and individual words in the list have no emotional or visual impact. The two words you are almost sure to remember are "see" and "sea." While they are spelled differently, their sound is the same, and people remember by *repetition*. On Word List #2, you will probably recall between seven and nine of the words. (That's more than 10 per cent better than you did on Word List #1.) Why? Because not only were the words in the list closely associated with

WORD LIST # 1
SAID
PACK
ABLE
CORD
WORK
SEE
JUST
NEW
TURN
SEA

WORD LIST # 2
SUMMER
TREES
PARK
CHILDREN
BASEBALL
PEANUTS
ELEPHANT
CIRCUS
LION
HORSEMEAT

WORD LIST # 3
CHAIR
GRASS
TRUTH
WATCH
TRAY
FLOWER
BARMAID
WINDOW
WHEEL
APPLE

one another; each word was also associated with a visual image. People recall by *association.*

List #3: The *number* of words remembered is not important, but the specific words *are.* The words which you probably wrote down first are: "Apple, Watch, Barmaid, Chair, Grass." If you are in military service, "wheel" may replace one of the foregoing; if you're a gambler, "tray" may supplant one of the five I suggested as the ones you would recall. It is almost *certain* that you recalled "Apple," "Watch," and "Barmaid." You remembered "Apple" and "Watch" because they were accompanied by a visual aid. *Visual aids are important!* You remembered "Barmaid" because it was the only person in the list; *people are important!*

One of the interesting things about List #3 is that you are not likely to recall words which are associated with very important and meaningful ideas: In a group of twenty or more people, having this list *read* to them, less than five out of twenty will recall "Wheel" or "Truth." Yet the wheel is man's greatest invention, and truth is what all men are supposed to be seeking for. Why don't they recall these "important" words? Simply because nothing is done to *make* them important in the list. When these two words—or their synonyms—are repeated in the list, they will be remembered by eighteen out of twenty people. The same is true if they are accompanied by a visual aid. Now, hear this! *The importance of an idea is no guarantee that your listeners will remember it*—unless you do something to *make* them recall it.

So, show how your ideas are associated with one another; try to make your transitions as clear as possible to strengthen this association. Throw away irrelevant material. Use visual aids. Support your main points by using people in specific examples; your listener wants to know *who* did *what,* as well as *when, where* and *how* it was done. Advertising men know this. An advertisement for a facial cream will show a picture of Lottie

Astorbilt of Park Avenue, captioned "Miss Lottie Astorbilt of Park Avenue and Palm Beach uses OUR facial cream, and artists proclaim her complexion a dream!" A cigarette advertisement discloses that "Buzz Conroy, famous All-American halfback, smokes Weedies, and says, 'The tobacco in Weedies is mild and sweet; light up one and give yourself a treat!' "

During more than twenty years of teaching students in college and in industry, I have listened to thousands of speeches. Most of them I do not remember. However, I do remember many, many vivid *specific examples* that were used in those speeches. The reason for this is that we do not think in abstract terms but in concrete ones. If you call to mind any abstraction—goodness, justice, philanthropy, greed, malice, and so forth—you will find that you think of it in terms of *somebody doing something.* So, use case histories, stories, anecdotes to support your points. Notice how the late President Franklin Roosevelt uses a case history to support his point in the following selection from one of his speeches:

> I shall tell you what sold me on old-age insurance—old-age pensions. Not so long ago—about ten years—I received a great shock. I had been away from my home town of Hyde Park during the winter and when I came back I found that a tragedy had occurred. I had had an old farm neighbor, who had been a splendid fellow: Supervisor of his town, Highway Commissioner of his town—one of the best of our citizens. Before I left, around Christmas time, I had seen the old man, who was 89, his old brother, who was 87, his other brother, who was 85, and his "kid" sister, who was 83.
>
> They were living on a farm. I knew it was mortgaged to the hilt, but I assumed that everything was all right, for they still had a couple of cows and a few chickens. But, when I came back in the spring, I found that in the severe winter there had been a heavy fall of snow, and one of the old brothers had fallen on his way to the barn to milk the cows, and had perished in the snow drifts.

The town authorities had come along, and had taken the other two old men and had put them into the county poorhouse. They had taken the old lady and had sent her down—for want of a better place—to the insane asylum, although she was not insane, but just old.

That sold me on the idea of trying to keep homes intact for old people.

Limitation

Limit your number of points to those that will sell your idea; minor details can be brought out by questions from your listeners and answers from you. Let us suppose that Clem Abernathy is in the market for a new automobile. He has narrowed his choices down to two cars, the Swallow and the Gazelle. The two are in the same price range, are the same size, and have about the same performance records. With Clem, it's the flip of a coin to decide which to buy. However, in fairness to the competing salesmen of the two cars, he agrees to give each man fifteen minutes to talk with him before he makes up his mind.

The Swallow salesman spends his fifteen minutes showing Clem performance and durability records and other testimonials which give *twenty* reasons why the Swallow is the best automobile in its class. Clem is impressed, but will not announce his decision until tomorrow.

The Gazelle salesman also has records and testimonials which show why the Gazelle is superior in twenty ways, but *he doesn't use them* during his allotted fifteen minutes with Clem. He has learned that Clem is a "speed-demon" and that Clem's wife is a social climber. So, he uses his fifteen minutes with Clem to demonstrate how safe the Gazelle is at high speeds, how rapidly it accelerates ("From standstill to sixty miles per hour in thirty seconds"), its additional power for passing other cars on the road; he also shows Clem photographs of Lord and Lady Rearbumper with *their* Gazelle, and a picture and testimonial—gushing with praise for *their* Gazelle—from Senator and Mrs. Ritchgilt. Again, Clem is impressed, but says he wants twenty-four hours in which to make up his mind.

During the twenty-four hours in which he has to decide, which sales pitch will Clem remember most clearly—the one with twenty points, or the one with four? The answer is obvious.

Appeal for Action

You are now ready to "close the sale" by telling your listener what you want him to do. Do you want him to think or act in a certain way? Do you want him to buy something? Do you want him to vote for Senator Grabmore? Do you want him to change his mind about a city bond issue? Tell him so! In the two following excerpts, note how the speaker and writer get to the point; the first is from a speech delivered by Sir Pierson Dixon in the United Nations.

> It seems to me that the time has now come when the General Assembly must clearly put on record what it thinks about Soviet armed intervention in the internal affairs of Hungary, and must without any ambiguity reiterate its calls upon the Soviet Government to desist from such intervention.

> If you receive an offer that smells the least bit of fraud, take whatever documents you have received through the mail—*with the envelopes*—to your postmaster immediately. You may save not only yourself but perhaps a lot of others from being victimized. The postal inspectors have the facilities and the power to stop these evils which have grown up in recent years. But they need your help.[9]

You may take your appeal for action a step further and picture the rosy results of his action to your listener. This is some-

[9] Frederic Sonden, Jr., "Look Out for Larceny in Your Mailbox," *The Reader's Digest*, January, 1961. (Used by permission.)

times referred to as the "dawn-of-a-new-day" conclusion. In its crudest and most obvious form, here is such an ending used in a sales talk:

> These electronic kitchen ranges save labor, money and worry. When you buy this electronic range you enter into a new world of housekeeping: A world of no burnt fingers for you or for your children, for every point of likely contact is thoroughly insulated; a world of no rushing home from your Bridge Club to start dinner, for this range can be set to start and stop cooking automatically; a world in which cooking time is cut by as much as three hours a day, because of infrared heat. Three hours of leisure in which to read, play with the children, visit with friends—or loll luxuriously in a bubble bath and to put that extra curl in your hair that will put an extra glint in your husband's eyes!

In a more subtle way, Ben W. Heineman used the "dawn-of-a-new-day" ending in a public speech delivered in 1957:

> The stakes are high for all of us. But if we are successful, if the railroads are stripped down and made muscular, as I am confident they can be, they will perform their mass-transportation function more cheaply and more efficiently than has ever been known before. I see an industry that will be continuing to pay—not spend—tax dollars. Finally, I see an industry growing in volume, increasing its employment and growing in the service that it renders to the public.

In summary, you must get attention in order to arouse interest; you must sustain interest by appealing to the *listener's* needs; you must give your ideas impact by speaking in concrete terms and using visual, as well as verbal, aids; and you must *ask* for action, if you are to sell ideas successfully.

Index